Staying On Top In
Real Estate
THE PROFESSIONAL'S SUCCESS GUIDE

Karl Breckenridge

REAL ESTATE EDUCATION COMPANY
a division of Longman Financial Services Institute, Inc.

DEDICATION

. . .to Revis Edwards:
Friends don't get any better. . .

. . .to Rollan Melton:
*20th-century newspaper
columnist* extraordinaire,
and a Nevadan. . .

Publisher: Kathy Welton
Executive Editor: Wendy Lochner
Project Editor: Ellen Allen
Cover Design: Vito De Pinto

© 1990 by Longman Group USA

Published by Real Estate Education Company
a division of Longman Financial Services Institute, Inc.

Printed in the United States of America.

90 91 92 10 9 8 7 6 5 4 3 2 1

Library of Congress Cataloging-in-Publication Data

Breckenridge, Karl.
    Staying on top in real estate / Karl Breckenridge.
        p. cm.
    ISBN 0-88462-989-9
    1. Real estate agents. 2. Real estate business. 3. Success in business.   I. Title.
HD1382.B74 1990
333.33—dc20   89-39783
                                                                  CIP

Contents

Preface

After teaching real estate for five years at our local community college, we came upon the realization that the questions at the forefront of our first-night students' minds had very little to do with Nevada Revised Statute 645.001: REAL ESTATE BROKERS. Their truly meaningful inquiries revolved around "What happens when I go on vacation?" "Can I survive without a BMW?" and "Does Coldwell Banker allow a blazer with dolman sleeves?"

*   *   *   *

Recently, while poised at a career threshold rich in choices, we were faced with writing another real estate book or facing the music and brokering an actual real estate transaction. Owing consideration to the best interests of a potential buyer and seller, our state regulatory body and the industry as a whole, we opted to go for the book. The next choice was to give the industry yet another book steeped in the charisma, suspense and passion contained in N.R.S. 645 or to supply answers to new agents' questions that would prepare them to survive in the real world of real estate with knowledge seldom reduced to the printed word.

Having read and taught N.R.S. 645 and thereby knowing it definitely not to have the inspiration of a Clancy or a Ludlum, the preferable book theme became the non-statutory concerns of real estate as they embarked upon the business. As an instructor, we came to know that teaching real estate isn't a whole lot different from teaching our own kids to swim: if it's work, they sink like little bricks, but while it's just "funnin' around," they learn, ford the pool and then get a little miffed because you fooled 'em into doing something they had apprehensions about. The words that follow are just for recreation—you have a great career ahead of you. Now we're just splashing around the pool, but if you bob up at the other side with a few new ideas, good for you.

A rather irreverent passage here and there in the pages that follow may create the impression that the writer ascribes to no organized professional group recognizable by anyone in the real estate industry; but don't believe that for a minute. We are, in fact, proud of a long and active involvement in our local board of the National Association of RE-ALTORS®. (You'll read an occasional reference to the Code of Ethics of that Association.) We can't urge a first-year agent strongly enough to participate actively and soon in the local, state and national activities of the NAR.

$$* \quad * \quad * \quad *$$

We'll state very briefly the plight of the writer of a real estate book for a national audience: preferences and local practices vary. A Texan may conduct his or her practice differently from an agent in Vermont, but rest assured that we've probably talked to them both, and our words here represent the amalgamation of all of our ideas, across the land. But if we're way off-target for your area, let local custom prevail!

The time is upon us—let others speak of statutes, sealing wax and other fancy stuff—we have an appointment to meet some people in real-life real estate. We welcome you as a coworker and offer a heartfelt wish for good luck!

Note: The word "REALTOR" refers to a member of the National Association of REALTORS® who subscribes to its Code of Ethics.

1

The Name of the Game

A year or so ago, upon finding a twenty-dollar bill burning a hole in our Levis, we ordered a sweatshirt lettered for "BRECKINBRIDGE RELITY," the usual appellation given our little firm by 60 percent of our callers. It brought very few guffaws in relation to the broader criticism by those who took it as a travesty upon a respected profession.

A sense of envy welled up for our high-school-buddy-turned-veterinarian whose business card reads: "Jack O. Walther, D.V.M./ Taxidermist. Win or Lose, You Get Your Dog Back."

We accept that as empirical proof that vets are more fun than real estate agents.

*   *   *   *

Travel back in time to when you last heard a disk jockey promise two theater tickets or an exquisite meal to the first caller to identify Ronald Reagan's opponent in 1984, Randy Gardner's ice skating partner in the 1980 Winter Olympics or who was on third when Mighty Casey struck out.

While you pounded your forehead into the dashboard trying to shake loose names imbedded there, you heard the jock echo the response of some lucky theater-goer or diner and wondered how you could ever have forgotten Walter Mondale, Tai Babylonia and Flynn (first name unchronicled).

Our introductory chapter and the one that follows revolve around the truth that an agent who helps a couple purchase a home endures in their memory about as long as any other once-household name that eventually fades into oblivion. And while Flynn was stranded when Casey struck out way back in 1888, the other two names rose to fleeting prominence as recently as the 1980s, quite possibly since the buyers purchased their home through you.

In the next pages, we'll try to find ways not only to increase name remembrance but to make the mere whisper of our name suggest "real estate."

*   *   *   *

The most obvious topic in chapters about visibility is the common denominator that we all arrive in business bearing: a name. Names are fun things; studies tell that few of us would pick our own again if given a choice. Many of us share our name with others, and occasionally we change our name in midcareer. Some agents have names nobody can pronounce or that can be spelled in a variety of ways in a phone book.

We'll not advocate changing whatever name you're currently using—that's a choice of your own, and our track record is poor. Two decades ago we probably would have urged a young basketball player with a sheepskin from UCLA and a killer skyhook to stick with Lew Alcindor because nobody would ever remember the name that he wanted to use in the NBA. Funny, but Kareem probably wouldn't have thought much of using "Karl Breckenridge" in a real estate career, either.

We can be brief on a few pointers: the first is to search your new market area for duplicate (or similar) names. In our area we have two brokers, Bill Myers and W. S. (Bill) Meyer—both active in association functions and good guys. The locals have learned to seek a singular or plural "Myer," but if you were starting your career here and thereby destined to become Bill the Third, you might want to go back to a high school nickname or a middle name.

Two words convey 95 percent of the second pointer: "Detective Wojo." Regional differences in name recognition persist. Few Westerners could pronounce or spell Barney Miller's sidekick's full name although it would be no problem in one of Chicago's affluent Polish neighborhoods. And, an Easterner might say uncle to the family name Marcueirquiaga, known well by us closer to America's Basque heartland. The message here falls short of a suggestion to change a family name, but try to recognize that some names are just toughies and may need a phonetic spelling on a business card. We'll hand out a few business cards in pages to follow.

*   *   *   *

The Addams Family noticed a spooky occurrence: You might have noticed on TV that their phone seldom rang, due largely to the fact that the things that went bump in the night looked for "Adams" in the directory and could never find them. Many business people, and indeed businesses, have shown a trend toward multiple listings in telephone and other directories. Names such as Addams and Smyth and Browne are excellent candidates for and examples of the need for a second listing, wherein John Smyth bites the bullet and caves in to the conventional spelling of his family name. The second listing's cheap, and one prospect call could pay for a career of extra listings.

The name recognition phenomenon that looms most prominently in our industry usually occurs during the typical American honeymoon, when Miss Smith, who spent five years building a faithful real estate clientele, opens her dreamy eyes and realizes that she's now Mrs. Jones. By law she must change her driver's and real estate licenses, but the overnight disappearance of Smith from the face of the earth, to be replaced by a newcomer named Jones, could deliver a fatal blow to the Smith/Jones career.

There's no right or wrong tactic for a name transition, and some may see no need for a transition at all. One of the classiest and busiest offices in our town bears the maiden name of a broker who met her groom at the end of the aisle a decade ago and just never bothered to change her firm's name. Other licensed brides have recycled the surname with which their good business reputation was established into a middle name for a period of time, a year or so, until the world became accustomed to the new name. At some point, the former name may be phased out without fanfare.

An alternative is to adopt a hyphenated former-present surname, reminiscent to many of us, at least out West, of a 1950's sports car or the stuffy armorer in a James Bond movie.

The Firm's Name

So far in these pages the discussion has been of personal choices and elective changes or alterations of our monikers, but at this point we'll make the observation that whatever name you settle on, in a small sense becomes cast in stone, or at least in a computer disk, with your state real estate licensing agency. The next paragraphs deal with the proper use of that name.

To keep the discussion totally in proportion, it's probably wise to move up one layer in the name hierarchy, to the regulations governing your broker. And, in time-honored fashion, we preface the thought by stating that we're guided by the preponderance of legislation and statutes in all 50 states. Slight technical and semantic variations exist, but in spirit our words hold true.

In our state, and most others, an aspiring broker journeys to the county recorder and files a "Certificate of Fictitious Name," establishing sole right to a chosen name and preventing others from registering a duplicate or any variation that might confuse a resident of the county or injure the broker's business. That certificate, together with another seven pounds of paperwork, a small amount of cash and, in our state, our fingerprints, travels to Carson City where our licenses are issued.

The name selected on the fictitious name certificate may be an individual's name or any other word(s) to be used by the firm as a name. And that is the name that will thereafter forever be used by that firm and its licensees wherever the firm's name is displayed or disseminated publicly within the state. And it must be displayed *identically* as submitted—woe be to Grace if the Grace L. Ferguson Storm Door and Real Estate Company advertised over the name "Ferguson Realty."

Like most other one-person firms, we know the above rule all too well from occasionally having had our wrist slapped for simply using our given name in place of the requisite "Breckenridge Realty."

A few more thoughts about broker firm names, applicable in most states: A franchise name, e.g., Red Carpet or Century 21, is not included in the state's recognition of the individual firm name. A separate agreement between the franchiser and the broker enables the broker to use the franchiser's name in advertising. State practices vary as to the ratio of size and visual impact of broker name versus franchise name in advertising display. At one time most states would not allow the franchise name to "dominate" the display, also expressed as "exceed a fraction of," (usually one-half) the sign. The trend is now to allow an attractive integration of broker name into nationally recognized franchise advertising.

A few minor notes about franchised licensees. Most states require a broker to advise their state agency that they participate in a franchise. And most state agencies, through statute, protect registered franchised brokers from unauthorized use of the franchise name by non-member brokers. Final "most": Most states require the phrase "Each Office Independently Owned and Operated" to appear in conjunction with any public display of a franchise name.

*   *   *   *

Still holding your employing broker in the bright beam, a final point should be made about names, and this one isn't in the individual state's jurisdiction—it rests with the National Association of REALTORS®. We make reference in this book to the NAR only sparingly, but in this case we hope they'll welcome our statement of their preference. The preference (make that *rule!*) is that the word "REALTOR®" not be integrated into a firm's license name, and many state bureaus honor the NAR's request by not recognizing such a name. You will, from time to time, see the registered tradestyle used improperly in a broker's advertising. (Another aspect of this prohibition is probably within the purview of the county recorder: A fictitious name filing can't be used to protect a tradestyle already "owned" by another entity.)

A preference or statute that may apply in your state is the obligation to disclose license status in advertising. We'll have more to say on this subject in later paragraphs about individual licensee requirements.

Many states require that any display of information intended to motivate a member of the public to buy real property *must* contain some variant of the phrase "Licensed Real Estate Broker." And some states recognize the tradestyle "REALTOR®" as a substitute. The intent is that a lay person, responding to a phone number in an ad or a yard sign, will be advised that he or she is dealing with a licensed person charged with a higher knowledge of real estate law and ethics. Regrettably, some states do not require this procedure, and others that required it in the past have softened up or removed the obligation in an effort to conserve space and cost of newspaper advertising.

We would hope that our readers will share our pride in our profession and continue to use the phrase, required or not. We worked hard to get the license, and buyers and sellers, in the long run, like to work with professionals.

The Individual's Name

Stepping down now from that brief interlude on our soapbox, we'll move right along to you, the reader, who was given or otherwise has now chosen a name with a pleasant ring to it. Let's bond it legally to your broker's name and turn it into a marketing tool.

One of the first purchases most new agents make as the ink is drying on their licenses is their business cards. These cards form the foundation of most of our client contact—we hand them out to virtually everyone we come in contact with, we overlay them in a photocopy machine to create letterhead on fliers, we laminate them in plastic to make luggage tags and name badges. (And we're usually out of them when we need them most!)

Slight digression: Use just a little discretion in handing out cards helter-skelter—they're not a mass marketing tool to be dropped from an airplane over Yankee Stadium. Your name may be "adopted" by a bad guy and your card used to verify his/her identity. Suggestion: Order cards with your photo on them; many offices are adopting this as a policy.

We write in the context of business cards, but hand-in-hand with business cards come sign "riders" for yard signs, magnetic car signs, inclusion of your name in rosters and other license-mandated printed matter—in short, anywhere your name appears.

The message: Display your name as it appears with your state agency or face the eventuality of starting over again. State regulators periodically grow weary of regulating a stateful of nicknames and crack the whip on the Bozos, FiFis and P.J.s.

Some common sense and knowledge of your own state's lenience is required here—few states would get too excited about Frederic becoming "Fred" or Susan opting for "Susie." But crossing over the line too far might bring a warning. Frederic using "Rick" could put him at loggerheads with a "Richard" across town, ditto "Susie" and "Suzy." It's best to look at your nickname from all perspectives, and you are hereby forewarned that there are a few states where Susan is "Susan," period.

But if J.D. Salinger, Flojo, Chuck Yeager and Huey Lewis can buy business cards any way they want, then we affirm that we can, too, as long as the dominant line agrees with the name on our license. On a following line, generally in lighter and/or smaller type and in quotation marks, you're free to be "Bozo" if you so desire.

The companion thought is that a phonetic spelling of a tough name be included on your card—for example "So-Sha" on a line below "Mike Scioscia," if the artful Dodger were to forsake home plate to catch on in home sales.

*   *   *   *

With a reminder that we're conveying a consensus of all 50 states' regulations, and yours may depart slightly, we'll take the name on that business card, flier, sign rider, whatever, and bring it into focus with the rest of the artwork.

You saw a clue in earlier text: Just as the franchise name could not dominate the broker's name, your name cannot dominate your broker's name. This is a sticky wicket due to semantics and the spirit of the regulations where they apply. Some states continue to mandate that the broker's name must be larger than the agent's, although through halftones and bold colors, the smaller-type agent's name can wind up dominating the larger-but-subdued firm name.

A prevailing and more workable regulation simply requires that the firm name must not be dominated by the agent's name, and a tie is usually OK.

You'll probably find upon joining your new office that the business card process is pretty well defined and that your name will be inked onto an established format. The above few paragraphs acquire importance as you begin coming up with your own advertising tools and tricks, e.g., fliers for open houses and listings, and as you start ordering custom outdoor signs and newspaper advertising. At these junctures, you may want to run the ad copy or sign art by your manager to confirm that they remain within office policy and state regulations.

*   *   *   *

One area where all of us who work in tightly regulated states occasionally step out of the beaten path is in the so-called "institutional" ads we sometimes place—often as a donation to Public TV or a school PTA carnival. These are usually designed to advertise ourselves, not one specific piece of property.

It's very easy for "Veronica Lodge, Real Estate Sales" to wind up being enumerated in a roster of opera singers or high school football team supporters. And there are in this world a number of stuffed shirts (usually competitors!) eager to mail off the offending football program to the state licensing authorities.

The point is to try to ensure that any representation of your name in a business capacity, to be circulated in even a limited way, be done within the requirements of your state. The line between a generic identification of your profession and an interpretation of advertising or promoting it is faint indeed.

Spoken Disclosures

A final look at the use of your name in the context of legality concerns an area harder to control because regulatory language addressing non-print disclosure is usually less clear in state statutes and often is interpreted more by inference than by text. Also, inappropriate behavior by an agent is harder to analyze or criticize—we're dealing now with the spoken word—fleeting syllables uttered once and, unless someone is lurking around with a tape deck, gone forever.

We can make this text short and sweet: If you're talking real estate, start the conversation with "I'm a real estate agent."

The legality is rooted in "Full Disclosure," capitalized to elevate it as a basic tenet of our profession. Clients and prospects, face-to-face or on the telephone, are entitled to know of our license status at the outset of any communication, just as they are in printed correspondence.

Concealment of that status, accidentally or by design, is an ominous pathway to major grief further down the line in a transaction. Granted, a prospect may hold back a bit when talking to a known licensee, but that early reticence is preferable to inducing a person to turn his or her hole card by withholding your license status.

But we don't stop with members of the public. Arguably, the real estate licensing laws of the various states are for the protection of the public, but a broad cross section of the industry holds that ''the public'' is non-severable with ''the industry.'' The conclusion to be drawn is that we're entitled to be protected from ourselves, and the tenet of license status disclosure is usually extended to include communication among agents and other parties to the transaction.

You'll probably have a long, happy and fulfilling career in real estate by just letting the whole world know up-front that you're in the business. And avoid the pitfall one novice agent fell heir to a year ago in our town:

An aging real estate writer spent ten minutes on the phone one Monday night pitching his listing and missed the goal-line fumble, a 49er TD, the replay and a Lite beer commercial. He learned only too late that the slam-dunk ''buyer'' on the phone was in reality a novice agent with a potential buyer coming to town on *Wednesday*.

The 'Niners won it all at Super Bowl XXIII—the deceptive agent won only a dressing down, and he is still grinding out short yardage deep in his own territory.

*   *   *   *

We had a bit of fun in the early pages of this chapter, but much needed to be said about the legal and ethical usage of names. With the hard work now behind us, we can go back to a more relaxed brand of reading. In the companion chapter that follows we'll try to get our name known to all the buyers and sellers who are just waiting for the right agent to ride into town.

2

The Game of the Name

One of the more reliable freebie ways to get our name bandied around publicly is to sign up with the hostess for dinner at the Nugget casino in Sparks (East Reno). On a good Saturday night a thousand local folks hear the page, "Breckenridge party of two to the Roundhouse Room," and they know we're still alive and tryin'.

*   *   *   *

Having used the last chapter to engender sufficient guilt, trepidation and uncertainty about the use and display of your own God-given name to last several months into your new career, we'll reveal in the early pages of this chapter that it is possible to have a little fun and use that name without looking over your shoulder for a licensing officer. We'll look at three types of tactics to keep your presence in the business community alive: Highly visible but nonlicensed activities in the community; mailings targeted toward previous clients; and house-warming presents calculated to keep your name known long after the escrow closes.

The premise for the initial stratagem is that human nature compels all of us to want to know what an accomplished or otherwise interesting person does for a living. Check out our theory: If you hear a soprano hit G over high C in an amateur opera or read of a golfer winning an amateur match with a double eagle, your natural curiosity might lead you to wonder what these people do in real life.

There are probably several levels on which this curiosity can be turned to your advantage. The first is just plain doing what you enjoy doing, on a slightly more visible basis than you once did it, and letting the world find out that you're an interesting person—an interesting person with a real estate license. And if your endeavor lands you in the news, more's the better. Journalists *love* occupations. We allude to this in another chapter about affinity farming, and we reiterate that the less said about real estate and the more effort given the leisure endeavor, the greater the rewards probably will be, personally and in business. Which is not to say that if you're in the annual 5K run, your Coldwell Banker cap won't keep the bright sunshine out of your eyes!

Most of us live and work somewhere on that level of visibility. One rung up the ladder are the agents with a flair for the dramatic, a touch of the showboat or possibly an athletic accomplishment that might cause a hero-hungry world to seek them out. (A perennial winner of the Reno National Championship Air Races sells real estate during the other 51 weeks of the year.)

We mentioned fellow broker and *bon vivant* Bill Myers early in the previous chapter. When Bill takes his banjo band to the local Senior Center, the words "real estate" are never uttered. But rest assured that the legionnaires in the assembled Gray Power squadron can't wait to tell their sons and daughters that young Billy Myers is the *only* person to call on about their real estate needs.

The Legend Lives

The promontory on the escalating scale of Becoming Known is the out-and-out stunt, in some rare cases almost approaching legality.

Witness: A fine pillar of the community named Harry O'Brien once paid annual homage to his Emerald Isle ancestry by pulling a few corks late in the evening of each March 16th preparatory to dispatching a band of leprechauns to downtown Reno, where they would then repaint the white line down the middle of the main drag a bright Kelly green.

The so-called Smilin' Irishman's competition lay awake nights for a decade trying to figure out how to bring this civic vandalism to a halt before the adoring townsfolk virtually deified Harry. His detractors finally realized that it was better to join than to fight him, and they chipped in to buy him more paint.

Harry went to his reward, like many Irishmen, too early, but the reader may be assured that the caper lives on, and at daybreak of each St. Patrick's Day, Reno's casino row is still a 'wearin' the green.

*   *   *   *

The moral of all these thoughts is that people, the ones residing in your market area from whom you will draw your growing client list, learn early that you're in real estate and for the most part could give a tinker's dam about your 20 post-license hours of continuing education.

But be the neighbor who can teach their daughter a pike one-and-a-half dive with a half-twist or their son how to catch a knuckleball from a lefty, or the person who coaches a Special Olympics athlete, sneaks a Scott Joplin rag out of the Episcopalian Hammond or sky-dives into the Homecoming game with a Century 21 banner attached to his 'chute's canopy, and you'll probably get more phone calls earlier in your career than the dullard novice who can afford a half-page introductory ad in the local paper.

Direct Mail

We depart now from activities and adventures targeted toward introducing you to the community and go to the second entree promised on the menu: Correspondence, usually by mail, to known persons. In the chapter introduction we identified these people as former clients, but that list would be rather short for fairly new agents, so we'll leave that language on hold for a few paragraphs and go to plan B.

Observe, if you will, a postcard, (page 13), 3½" by 5½", on fairly stiff paper and dove gray in color.

We invite and challenge the reader to make the vow we made back in 1973 or 1974 to mail at least two of these cards each and every business day to someone—to a friend, to a local superstar who made the morning news (or the superstar's parents), to a fellow agent who showed one of our listings or deserves to hear our prospect's reactions.

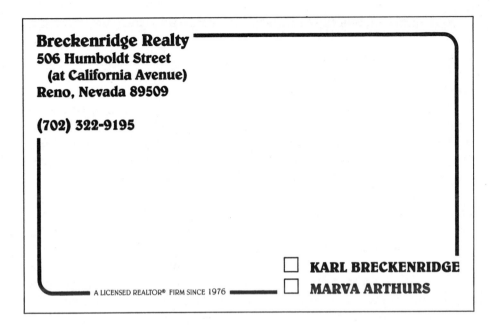

Cards are nifty things. They're cheap to mail and small enough to slide into an envelope (pre-stamped and self-addressed) to facilitate a response. And you can carry a few in your glove box or purse to give to people who want to get back to you. Note that we disclose on them our state license status just in case one gets in the hands of a party who doesn't know that we're licensed.

Postcards are nonthreatening to the recipient—they don't have to be opened, and given the volume of mail we get in this business, envelopes that need opening can easily be pushed aside for other activities. Their small size and rigidity make them logical candidates to be slid into a datebook or kept on a bulletin board or refrigerator door.

We lay no claim to originating the idea but have used it with success for many years. Occasionally, we see one of our aging postcards in a friend's office or home, with an "attaboy" or some other message that seemed terribly profound when we wrote it. We assume that at least several other people saw the card and then learned that accounts of our demise were greatly exaggerated. And that, with apologies to Samuel Clemens, is the game of the name.

*   *   *   *

As your circle of business contacts increases and your prospect list transforms into one of clients, you might find yourself wanting to utilize first-class mail, where your message, for a slight postal premium, may be placed *inside* of an envelope, away from the prying eyes of everyone in your friend's office.

We won't bore you with where to find note paper, but since we commit the fallacy in the upcoming "Records" chapter of endorsing Day-Timers for use as pocket calendars, you might as well order some of their boxed personal stationery at the same time. It's attractive stuff, and you can save writing another check.

Some communications are best keyed around a calendar year. Cards during the Holidays are nice and require little comment other than to call attention to the word "holiday," a word with no sectarian connotation and pleasant for business friends of all faiths. Birthdays are nice, but greetings can be a bit cumbersome when many parties are involved. A real natural in our business is the anniversary of home ownership, and we've found that our friends get a kick out of realizing just how long they've lived there! (You'll use some of the resources we mention in the "Records" chapter to organize this campaign.)

A recurring dilemma with all business people is to gauge when an apparently personal greeting crosses the line into a thinly cloaked commercial solicitation; or, restated, when does a solicitation arriving within a personal Trojan Horse start irritating a client?

Most of us can only use our own emotions and responses as a barometer. We personally enjoy the birthday card from our insurance agent, even with the annual handwritten tweak about our advancing years. But if each October 20th brought a "Happy Birthday and let's review your life coverage," we'd probably soon part company. We apply this line of thought to our own communications with clients: "Happy tenth-year in your home!" from a friend, not a broker.

The Gift

Third on our agenda of definable methods to get and keep our persona in the forefront of previous clients' minds (and maybe produce a referral or two) is a gift, a housewarming remembrance, delivered with great flourish and aplomb *after* the buyer/clients have settled in. A fancy gift plopped among a van-load of packing boxes, ficus trees and trikes somehow loses the essence of its intent.

And a point should be made, this on a downer note, then we'll put it behind us: You'll hear it said, probably by a failing practitioner, that a post-escrow closing gift to a homebuyer from an agent who received compensation from the *seller* constitutes a rebate. Some aberrated logic crops up every so often to reprove this theory, and we suppose that if you are putting a new 'Vette in the buyer's garage with your business card taped to the tach, the theory might ring true. But few homebuyers would move kit and kaboodle into a new home with the sole expectation of being given a picture of the home in a shiny new brass frame at closing.

*   *   *   *

Now, along to the brighter side of gifting the pair of impersonal home-buyers that you met many months ago in a crowded airport and who have since become humans—friends, with children, parents, hobbies, just like us, and a need to assimilate into their new town. And, of course, they arrived with butterflies, anxieties and trepidation about their move.

If you become like most veteran agents, you'll learn that although we try hard to get that which is the only thing that distinguishes us from the competition, our name, out to the public, the drive for publicity takes a back seat to friendship at close of escrow. With some difficulty, we put aside the truth that we in fact (usually) owed fiduciary obedience to the seller, and a housewarming gift, if we offer one, almost always is from the heart.

But from the heart also come the words of many pages ago, revealing that after a period of years, recollections tend to dull a bit. As agents, we frequently have to rely on old files to remind us who bought what house from whom and for how much. And if we, who do it for a living, can't keep it all straight, we can scarcely expect the buyers and sellers, with a lot more on their minds during a move than our name, to do any better.

*   *   *   *

So, many of us offer a housewarming gift, with a tastefully subtle or concealed greeting, which the homeowner might see once or twice a year when the thing gets dusted or moved. It may be tailored to the homebuyers, aligned toward their taste for barbecuing or gardening. Or it may be oriented to the locale—a watercolor of the peak they can see from their new living room. The gift probably won't be obtrusive or committed to a specific decor, thereby likely consigning it to the basement or a garage sale. A comfortable, middle-of-the-road gift will be around for a long time to come.

But who are we to tell a reader how her tastes should run? It's a personal choice and one you will enjoy fulfilling as each new escrow closes. Our own choice of gift has caused a few soft hearts to palpitate over the years: As a devout sentimentalist of the romance-is-not-dead genre, we struck upon fire extinguishers as gifts early in our career. Not a little spray-can size extinguisher, mind you, but a good-sized appliance for a furnace room or garage. We adorn the tank with our office name and telephone number imprinted on a metallic foil label and whenever possible mount it in the garage before the buyers move in.

We gave half a dozen of them away with a card, ''Happy Housewarming from the Breckenridge Kidde,'' before the first buyers finally saw the irony of a fire extinguisher for a housewarming gift and noted that Kidde was the manufacturer.

They aren't pretty but they're durable, and many of them have been around for a decade or more, long after a house plant gift would have gone to hydrangea heaven. And that's the beauty of longevity—a 1970's homebuyer, now ready to sell, can look at the thing and remember that Breckenridge is *the* one to call.

Or is it Kidde?

*   *   *   *

As advertised, we've served up three vehicles designed to generate business. We embellished them, dolled them up and threw in a little levity, but when all's said and done, they still sort out to a high-profile civic and community involvement and diligent pursuit of correspondence. The third strategy is less a business generator than what might be called a rite of passage, but in the right context it brings great pleasure to both you and your clients.

But don't stop with these vehicles—if you have another, play it out. We've only scratched the surface of the motivators that bring business our way. The one and only generalization we'll offer—that we defy you to dispute—is that after a decade in the profession if you're having a great time and making a new contact every day that you go to work, you've probably become a success!

*   *   *   *

These ''name'' chapters began on a canine note, so it seems appropriate that we leave them in similar fashion before embarking on to the next topic at hand.

Since you've made it this far into these pages, you obviously qualify as the bibliophile sort, so we'll impart a closing veterinary/literary truth from Doctor Jack:

> ''Outside of a dog, a book is a man's best friend.
> Inside of a dog, it's too dark to read.''

3

Compensation

Words can be fun. Congregate fifty or sixty thousand of them into some sequence and you'll own a book that will teach or amuse you all night long. Or ponder an interesting word such as bookkeeper—*the only word in the English lexicon that contains three pairs of double letters in sequence. Just fascinating!*

Another is eleemosynary. *The letters alone are worth 20 Scrabble points, not counting bonus squares and assuming that you could play it. But it's not a word we associate with real estate. It indicates a motivation inspired by charity, which is not why we do what we do. We're motivated by words such as* f-o-o-d, m-o-r-t-g-a-g-e *and* t-u-i-t-i-o-n, *not bad in Scrabble but triumphant in the board game of life.*

*   *   *   *

We taught real estate principles and practices at our local community college for half a dozen years before a student posed this question point blank: How does a real estate agent get paid?

It seemed a fair question, yet not one answered clearly and directly in our texts. We make many assumptions while teaching—we assume that all know that we work speculatively, for commission. That's not a bad generalization, but it stops far short of explaining many nuances of the profession. We'll explore that oversimplification for a few paragraphs and then let the text go off in a starburst of directions.

*   *   *   *

First, the ground rules: We're writing to the broader mainstream of fairly new agents and their managers. If the words don't seem to apply to you, to your office or to your marketing area, read on anyway. Your locality's practices, if applicable to a majority of beginners, may be integrated into the text in later pages.

And let's achieve some commonality of thought about the key word of this chapter: Commission. We write of that term as a percentage of conveyance price of a piece of real property. Don't tangle it up with any conditions other than that—we'll do that for you throughout the chapter!

The final ground rule addresses the source of the funds that we're accounting for. Compensation by the seller is the norm of the industry—but buyer agency is Topic A in every book and magazine across the land. (That concept will emerge and be better defined later.) For purposes of this chapter, we're confining the text to earned funds, with little or no regard as to whether they were provided by the sellers or the buyers.

Commissions Are Negotiable!

We suppose that to court the continuing favor of the U.S. Department of Justice, the National Association of REALTORS®, the 50 state regulatory agencies, Better Business Bureaus, HUD, and apple pie we should open the chapter with a statement to emboss on your dashboard and tattoo on your dominant upper extremity: *COMMISSIONS ARE NEGOTIABLE!* As you go forth in your career, you will have growing reason to wonder whether there are more investigators trying to catch or entrap an agent into erroneously representing that a commission is fixed by statute than there are agents just trying to get through the day and make a living.

The very simple fact is that a new agent should develop a Pavlovian tic in their speech to prevent their lips and tongue from forming words such as *usual, customary, accepted, normal, typical* and a dozen like words into the same sentence with the word *commission.*

We'll not consume a lot more paper and ink on the subject. You'll hear much more about the federal prohibition on a steady basis, and, in all sincerity, it's a vital and necessary campaign. If you're lucky, the now-famous audio tape will come to your town. On this engineering masterpiece two gentlemen, both likely rejects from the "Smokey and the Bandit" sound lot, converse on a telephone line with a recorder beeping in the background. The good guy, a pseudo-seller, tries to extract from the scoundrel licensee an admission that there is a "statutory" fee charged by all agents in the area. The agent, no fool, skirts the issue but finally drops his guard. The conclusion of the tape is reminiscent of Butch and Sundance's final moments in Bolivia. Great stuff, coming soon to a seminar near you.

A Fee Is Born

Having now perpetuated the forces of truth, justice and the American way in the community, we'll talk a little of compensation.

The initial link in the compensation chain is anchored by the listing contract, wherein the seller promises to deal exclusively with the brokerage firm and to compensate the firm, usually upon conveyance. The firm's agent, swapping a promise for a promise to create a bilateral contract, agrees to exercise "diligence" in securing a ready, willing and able purchaser.

Analysis: "Exclusively" connotes the nature of the listing contract, not grist for this chapter. Note that the "firm" receives the compensation, not the agent; note further, the contract thus created is the property of the firm. If the agent leaves the firm, the contract remains with the firm in the absence of another agreement. Final note: In the purest form of brokerage practice, and in most states, the broker executes the contract. In some areas brokers retain that obligation or yield it only to selected agents. In others, a salesperson is granted thinly supervised and unwritten authority to bind the broker to the obligation.

Within the constraints of our compensation chapter, we'll not dive too deeply into the contract's language. We will point out that there are blank spaces on most variants of listing contracts wherein a fixed dollar amount or a percentage of the conveyance price is to be specified. In usual practice, the dollar blank is "not applicable'd" and a percentage is entered.

Food for thought at this point often is the value and extent of personal property to be conveyed with the home. Small bells peal in sellers' minds when they realize that the brokerage cost for selling real property is increased by the inclusion of significant personal property with the home. The flip side is that selling the personal property may consume some of your time and expertise, for which you are entitled to be compensated.

Just a thought.

*   *   *   *

A few blanks down in the boilerplate language of the contract, your form might indicate some variation of "Fee/Commission of $____/ ____% to be paid if home is conveyed within _____ days of expiration of listing. Broker to provide seller a list of prospects within _____ days of expiration." (Language abridged.)

What's happening here is a protection for the broker. It blocks a prospect from seeing the home a day before the listing expires and, although the procuring cause chain is still intact, having the seller go directly to the prospect and deal around the broker. Many brokers who use this form insert the commission in the blank and protect themselves for 30 days following expiration.

Early in your career you might expect a cooperating broker, through an MLS system, to request that you inform your principal (the seller) that so-and-so was shown the home and that her brokerage firm asserts a right to cooperating commission in case so-and-so or the sellers try an end run around the system. We then advise the sellers, in writing, of so-and-so's possible interest.

*   *   *   *

Time marches on, and the next few thoughts are a pleasure to write and read: Buyers are found, their money is placed into an escrow account and on the day of close of escrow (COE, in some circles) the closing agent multiplies the sale price by the commission you agreed upon so many months ago and writes a check to your broker.

That little quickie paragraph forms the hub of a wheel with several spokes that we'll trace out in the next few pages.

The first spoke is as easy as the hub: Your broker, within a time frame expressly dictated in few states, writes a check to you for a percentage of the total commission received by the firm from escrow. That percentage is, in the vernacular of the business, your "split." Now pour a fresh glass of iced tea and get comfortable—that term is integral to your livelihood, and we'll take a long look at it.

The Office "Split"

There are probably as many "split" formulas as there are brokerage offices, about 134,000 nationwide at this writing. As a baseline, we'll just say that you have been offered, and have accepted, a "60/40" split—not bad for the first year. You keep 60 percent of what you bring into the office.

But we know of no way to totally express the value of this split by only reciting two percentages totaling 100. Ask further when you're interviewing with an office: "What does the 40 percent buy?" There are 134,000 variations of who pays for advertising, desk fees (rent, in effect, on your desk), telephones, business cards, listing input fees, postage, E&O (errors and omissions) insurance, photocopies, yard signs and tools of the trade *ad infinitum*. We've heard of agents on an 80/20 split that are near starvation after the "80" is invaded by office bills.

Following the interviewing broker's explanation of potential charges against your split, another discussion might be of split thresholds—the production level when your share of the split might be increased. These motivational plateaus are employed by many offices to keep veteran producers active beyond that time of the year when they hit their desired level of subsistence and cave in to the siren cry of the golf course or a shopping mall.

*   *   *   *

Some offices adjust their split thresholds to sales dollar volume and others tie them to actual revenue produced. Variation 1: An agent may start her year on a 50/50 until she closes $1 million in sales volume. She might then step up to a 75/25 for the balance of her year. In another office all associates might start their year at 55/45, with an agent seeing the brighter side of 75/25 after he brings $12,500 total commission through the door. Two notes are appropriate here: Some offices have more than one level, e.g., 50/50 to 60/40 then, after more production, another step up to 75/25 just to keep all on their toes. Secondly, offices seem to favor the commission-produced threshold over sales volume. A salesperson knocking on the door to go from $50/50$ to $80/20$ for the rest of the year might be inclined to slam-dunk a simple transaction for little or no commission if a blockbuster commission were just around the corner.

*   *   *   *

Housekeeping item: Most offices restart the basic, lower split for each agent annually. Agents who've had a decent prior year may not plumb the full depths downward to the beginning scale but can expect a little "bump" to get their priorities refocused.

Variation II in the science of splits is a factor used by some offices to motivate agents to look first for suitable in-house listings before taking buyers out into the MLS inventory. The factor is frequently applied to whatever split an agent may be getting, as in "split times 125 percent," or it may be an upward adjustment of the split: $60/40$ adjusting to $65/35$ for an in-house sale. Interesting question: Does the premium bonus apply to the selling portion of the commission if an agent sells her own listing?

In months and years to come, we'll all know more about buyer agency—and in some states we'd better learn it pronto. Look for a redefinition of the premium split for in-house sales. We're hampered by lack of experience in this emerging concept and the obvious difficulty of articulating that which we haven't experienced. But you read it here first: Salespeople acting as buyer's agents "steering" buyer/ principals to in-house listings that might generate higher revenue could inadvertently confuse their fiduciary obligation.

*   *   *   *

Variations I and II in the office split text might tend to confuse and overwhelm the newer licensee, but bear in mind that within the context of a single agent, we're dealing with pure math and recordkeeping. But when considering the splits of *two* cobrokering agents within an office, we find an apparent disparity due to the two agents' differing levels of production in his or her "year," or due to the fact that the selling agent receives an in-house bonus while the lister's share usually reflects no such premium.

But these two variations are in reality only the jumping-off point of sanity. Look now at 134,000 ways of apportioning a franchise fee, say 5 percent of the total commission (a random number). Frequently that amount departs directly from escrow to the franchiser, and the remaining 95 percent of the office's commission is subjected to the split. Or ponder the franchised office, already looking at a 5 percent bite, closing an escrow whose roots were in a relocation referral, with 10 percent of the commission (the office's net or the total?) subject to forwarding to the relo company.

Now, oblivious to outside entities, let's touch off a few meaningful discussions within our own office's walls: Picture in your mind's eye an agent who's at $^{50}/_{50}$ with $11,000 earned year-to-date, and she will go to $^{75}/_{25}$ when she earns $12,500. She's closing an escrow producing $5,000 soon. Will she receive 50 percent of the whole $5,000 or 50 percent of $1,500 plus 75 percent of the balance over her $12,500 threshold?

Don't reach for your Casio. We're talking an $875 difference.

The other recurrent squawk arises out of the agent's anniversary (frequently the date he or she associated with the firm) and whether the split at the time of sale applies (arguably when the work was actually done) or at the time of conveyance.

Back now to the mind's eye and our friend of a paragraph ago, with a new scenario: She's already hit big-time $^{75}/_{25}$ and awaits the same $5,000 commission. But the septic inspection flunks and ties up the escrow for 30 days, during which time her anniversary comes and goes, and she goes back to a $^{50}/_{50}$ split of the entire commission.

$1,250 this time. All her friends call her "Chuckles."

The Office Shares Expenses.

There is a myth outside the real estate industry that agents receive the commission that they bargain for in the listing. Wise old owls know that about the time the escrow holder leaves for the courthouse to record the deed that puts the commission in our pocket, the listing's electric garage door opener jams with the door half shut (or half open, if you're an optimist). And we find it's easier just to go to Sears and buy a new one than hold up the escrow over a minor deficiency.

Nickels and dimes we expect to spend, and a $35 porch light is an irritation but not life-threatening. But a $250 door opener when we're on a $^{75}/_{25}$ split costs the equivalent of $333, and that starts to get our attention.

The point is that in many situations, and particularly when your manager has been forewarned, the office will be willing to participate in an expenditure that facilitates a sale to the limit of their share of the split. In the same vein, it's sometimes wise to direct funds from escrow to meet such expenses, if time permits. Your accountant might agree that direct payment could clarify or reduce taxable income.

Using Commission As Down Payment

Our words now take a slight detour, and while the casual observer might interpret this as a departure from "split talk," you've no such luck—we're just setting the stage for the next act.

In times past, there existed a trend for a few people—coworkers, family, neighbors or the like—to band together, pool their resources and buy a little piece of property. Frequently, a real estate licensee was included in the investment group, inasmuch as he or she saw these affordable gems come on the market earlier than most and had a bit of expertise in acquiring property and in analyzing P&L statements. Further, the licensee could waive a commission (but contribute equally with the others) and purchase the gem sooner for less down. With ensuing changes in the tax codes, these partnerships now seem to be on the wane.

An adaptation of the investment group wherein the licensed member participates in kind with the others is a partnership with two or more folks, created to purchase and hold property for investment. But there's a twist.

If a reader has a friend she'd like to lose and nothing else seems to be working, try this: Find a piece of property that you could receive a $5,000 commission for selling. Then craft a purchase offer promising $10,000 down—the unrelenting friend's $5,000 cold cash and your $5,000 commission.

We'll virtually guarantee that when the friend later equates the ten paltry hours you spent on the conveyance to his or her 5,000 hard-earned dollars, the friendship will flicker and die.

But cotenancy lives on. And on. And, no, we don't sell the value of our expertise short. But associates, when comparing our skills with their dollars, sometimes do.

*   *   *   *

Back now to office splits, and not a moment too soon for many readers.

Our portion of a commission, that which would come to us at COE, is ours to be used as we see fit—as a bargaining chip in motivating a prospect to sign on the line or to waive from closing for reasons of our own. (A caution: Those who waive their portion of a commission in return for silent consideration from a buyer are known in the profession as ex-licensees.)

And now, the thrust of these paragraphs: Utilize full disclosure, and seek an opinion from your manager or broker regarding any contemplated departures from your usual office split percentage. Many brokers waive the entirety of the split due the office when an agent purchases a home to be used as a primary dwelling. Some waive, in full or in part, their split on land an agent is buying for construction of a personal residence. But few will care to subsidize an agent in revenue-producing endeavors, and rightfully so.

*   *   *   *

We're all back now to the hub of the wheel we created several pages ago, with only one minor note to include in the text before exploring another spoke. That note speaks of the reticence on the part of some brokers to employ an agent whose spouse is licensed with a competing firm. Arguments can be pursued that a conflict of interest exists, which might be the case, and could be aggravated by an unpleasant cobrokerage situation. But with our new-found "split" insight, conjure up a scenario wherein the licensed but competing married couple, he on $75/25$ in his office and she still at $50/50$ in hers, have friends who want to sell their home. Now predict for yourself who will take the listing.

Take that situation a step further and plug in the couples' anniversary date shifts, when he goes back to $60/40$ and she passes him up to $70/30$, and you'll soon realize why very few managers are willing to have a member of their sales team riding such a cyclical seesaw.

Some would say that when both are licensed in one office, the same opportunity to feed business back and forth to capitalize on similar situations also exists, but most managers won't get too excited so long as their office is retaining at least some of the revenue.

And in some offices such alliances are formally solidified by recognition of the couples' production and compensation as the effort of one entity.

*   *   *   *

Another spoke in the hub of compensation could easily take just as much print, but we'll stop well short of that by simply telling you to reread the last few pages and substitute ''fee'' wherever ''commission'' appears. Semantically, there's a difference, but it's thin: Commission seems to be tied to percentage of a value, and a fee is descriptive of an hourly, or unit, rate of compensation.

Generally, fees earned by a salesperson are earned under the aegis of a broker's license and therefore are subject to the same split concept. Two categories of departures from this assumption exist:

The first departure contemplates services performed by a licensee on behalf of a client, which services may in fact need no license from your state agency to perform. Examples of such services, in many states, might include limited property management activities or performing appraisals. (Caution: leasing requires a license in most states.)

However, your firm may assert a right to supervise and participate in your management and appraisal efforts. It's a valid presumption that you will use the good name and reputation of your firm in securing these assignments and that you will use firm resources, e.g., letterhead, tax roll information, telephone and copy machine, in performing the work that results in the fee. It seems equitable that the firm should be compensated by some form of a split.

(The good news is that most firms back off and withhold only a token amount. A full $^{60}/_{40}$ split could knock most of the incentive out of performing a $125 appraisal.)

Splits vs. Pass-Throughs

A second category of services that you will expect compensation for is covered in a later chapter about custodial listings on vacant properties. What you'll read, in a nutshell, is that you will often babysit the sellers' home after they've left town, for which you will be paid.

(You'll also sell the home for a commission, but that compensation's not germane to this segment.)

The type of work we're speaking of in this category is not the stuff of licensure. Periodically driving by the home, confirming that the furnace is working, arranging for landscaping care and vacuuming the swimming pool, for example, are not license-requisite activities, and they neither cost your broker one dime nor do they expose the office's reputation.

But the payment may well come at close of escrow, included in your commission check. The closing statement will show "$2,000 property maintenance, XYZ Realty; $3,200, brokerage fees, XYZ Realty." The forewarning: Confirm with your broker well in advance of closing that the $2,000 will come to you intact and the $3,200 will then be subjected to your normal split participation.

We'll jump the gun a little here, then expand the following text in both the custodial listing and recordkeeping chapters: Your sellers may leave money with you to be used in the maintenance of their vacant home. This might be for paying the lawn maintenance people and furnace oil suppliers, or for one-shot repairs or improvements. In either case we advise that any such sums be placed in your broker's trust account. Close of escrow, when your commission is distributed and you are compensated for custodial services, is the right time to make sure that the funds in trust are either disbursed to vendors or returned to the sellers, in either instance with a full accounting provided.

*   *   *   *

Compensation directly to a salesperson by an apparent principal is an iffy proposition. If you're contemplating performing services and being compensated by a principal, you might be well advised to make your broker totally conversant with the scope of your activities.

A suggestion: Your principal (assuming that a salesperson can have a principal!) might direct funds directly to your broker for eventual 100 percent pass-through to you.

Referral Compensation

From time to time a salesperson recognizes a desire, or an obligation, to transmit funds to another salesperson outside his or her own firm.

The obvious example is a "thank you" for a referral from a friend across the county who knows better than to sell on unfamiliar turf.

But prior to suggesting two methods to compensate that agent legally, let's avoid some hard feelings: If you've promised her 20 percent of your commission at close, be clear on whether that percentage is before or after splitting with your office. A parallel thought is to ask your manager what would happen if the shoe were on the other foot—would you get 100 percent of what her broker sent to your broker for you? If it's a small home, she's on $60/40$, you're on $70/30$ and both brokers assert their right to their full split, it might be more fun to take her out for a burger and a Coke.

But if a shred of worthwhile income seems probable, here are two methods a salesperson may employ to compensate another licensee; both require your broker's concurrence. The first way is to create a deduction from your office's share of commission from escrow proceeds, to be remitted by the escrow holder to your friend's broker firm. Your broker can authorize that on the commission instructions.

The second method is for your broker to send the referral fee to her broker, for distribution to her. Accurate recordkeeping should prevent taxable income from being imputed to you or your office.

*   *   *   *

Several quarts of iced tea ago we revealed that a former student asked how an agent gets paid, and it was that innocent question that unleashed most of the preceding insights. The insights, by the way, are far from complete. More sophisticated transactions coming up soon in your career will unveil a host of new dimensions to you. In a similar vein are the transactions you are compensated for over a period of time, secured by promissory notes and mortgages and occasionally complicated by salespersons transferring from one firm to another. Some of these situations can take so many paths that discussion here becomes unproductive—seek a little help from a veteran after you have specific facts about your first complex commission.

Most folks outside our business think that if we know enough to keep our head low during our backswing, to press hard because we're making four copies and that banks close at 5:30 on Fridays, all real estate agents will soon own a Learjet and condo at Aspen. Show them this chapter, and they might have a heightened regard for the intricacies of our industry!

4

Business Development

Prior to World War II, the herald on a Fortune 500 company's letter-head offered a proud insight into that company's chosen endeavor. There was never a question about what National Cash Register and Standard Oil sold or manufactured.

Then came the era of bold initials—old friends became "NCR" and "Esso." But another change piqued the interest of many real estate brokers. We learned that the employee promotion policy of one of the true heavyweights was "I've Been Moved."

*   *   *   *

Only one-tenth of 1 percent of the million or so real estate agents in America could pull off the stunt that follows, but such a rare lady worked in our town years ago. On an otherwise slow afternoon, sales-wise, she tuned out while driving a narrow country road and banged into the rear bumper of a slow-moving car. During the course of apologies both deep and profuse, she learned that her victims were moving to Reno, and indeed the reason for their pokey speed was that they were searching for a particular home for sale on a secluded back road.

Being a firm believer in the concept that when life hands one a lemon, one makes lemonade, she offered to lead the homeseekers on their quest. As luck would have it, the listing was in the MLS, she had her book with her and before the sun set that day, the prospects-turned-buyers held in their hands an accepted offer, including all the patio furniture and a new pair of tail lights.

*   *   *   *

We're not advocating the preceding anecdote as a ploy to be integrated into your inventory of business development techniques. The thrust of this chapter is to explore a few of the more pedestrian approaches that new agents rely upon to develop a clientele. The parallel message is to encourage you to allow your horizons to broaden beyond what's written here, should a tactic look legal, reasonably enjoyable, possibly productive and work to the detriment of no other human, licensed or otherwise.

Down on the Farm

Just to get our feet wet, we'll throw out the term "farming," a technique practiced in most parts of the country on a more or less organized basis, particularly in larger brokerage offices. A "farm" is a defined zone within the office's market area that has been assigned to one agent (sometimes *team* of agents, but within these pages a solo operation). Only that agent is allowed by office policy to solicit listings in that zone.

Very simple, one might say, how can such a pure arrangement merit more than a paragraph in a book? An agent has the right to contact the owners of all the properties between First and Fourth Avenue and Spruce and Goose Streets; no other agent in her office may distribute fliers, phone or make personal solicitations within that area. (Note: The zone she enjoys exclusive run of is only protected within her *own* office. The area is no doubt "farmed" by many other offices, and she will encounter their agents as they work the territory they have exclusive right to within their own office.)

As the agent assigned to that farm, you work it diligently. Success doesn't happen overnight or in a month or sometimes even in a year. But over a longer period of time, you grow to know the residents of the area on a first-name basis, you patronize their businesses, you sponsor the area's Pop Warner football program or elementary school Walk-a-Thon. As you walk your farm with area newsletters about babysitters, recipes and gardening tips, the referrals start rolling in.

Successful farmers are the first to hear of a transfer, inbound or out, thus picking up a listing or a prospect. There are also referrals—a resident of the farm may know someone selling a home well across town, and you get the first chance at listing it. Soon "second-generation" business starts to happen. One of the purest joys in our business is listing the home you once sold to first-time buyers and then selling them their second home. (A commission's always nice, but the realization that they came back to you for service is sweeter than the income the first time it happens to you!)

*   *   *   *

So, it's simple. Instead of charging all over town, we zero in on one area and spend our time there on an almost daily basis.

Now, as is our style, we'll muddy up the simplicity of the farm just a bit: Most offices using the "farm" concept protect the assigned agent insofar as contacts made to owners previously unknown to anyone in the office and prevent or discourage others within the office from attempting to create associations with farm residents.

But few offices take the practice so far as to prevent an agent who has an association created outside and/or prior to the scope of the farm from listing a home within another agent's farm area. Relatives obviously fall within this category, as do those who *bought* in the farm area through another agent. And there are farm residents who have a relationship with another agent through an "affinity"—we'll talk about that in pages that follow.

So, listing "rights" to a "farm" don't guarantee 100 percent of the listing business in that area.

The Dynasty

At this juncture we'll reveal a truth about an office with a well-organized farm system: The concept is at once one of the most successful tools in generating both individual agent and office business and one of the most equitable methods of apportioning business among an active agent roster. At the same time, it's a difficult concept for a manager to administer and perpetuate. Here's the explanation.

The up-side is obvious—agents are freed of keeping track of a large section of a town and may become totally conversant in their own farm. Solicitation and direct mail costs are minimized as market saturation without repetition is ensured. Agents may solicit freely without fear of stepping on a compadre's toes. And the office maintains a highly professional profile.

Now the fun begins for the manager, who soon realizes that a small dynasty has been built between First, Fourth, Spruce and Goose, with a highly territorial mood created. Alas, neighborhoods grow, and at some point demographics indicate that one agent cannot handle the influx of new owners efficiently. Woe be to the manager who must divide the area, subdivide the farm, so to speak, to maintain overall equity and coverage.

Mature farms occasionally take on the color of a proprietary fiefdom in favor of the salesperson who developed the area. We'll not take sides with the farmer who built the office's success and market share in a particular area or with the broker or manager of the farmer's office, under whose name the business was built. We have heard of cases in major metropolitan markets where farms were virtually for sale, seldom for money but for other consideration. The appropriateness or impropriety of this degree of control over an area by an agent is rightfully settled on a case basis, and we offer the insight only to indicate to the newcomer the production value of a farm and some of the dynamics a successful one may create.

*   *   *   *

In the normal course of human events, agents who have developed a successful farm, albeit short of the proportions of an NFL franchise as described above, occasionally leave the business, their office, mortal life or inevitably grow weary of the incessant demands that farming places on an agent. Most brokers hold that the farms their agents have developed become the province of the office to reassign, usually with transition help from the outgoing agent, who may or may not receive a part of future income from the farm as a referral fee for introducing the replacement agent to the farm's inhabitants.

Occasionally, upon the departure of an agent holding control of one of the office's more lucrative farms, a shift will be made by several agents, all ''bidding'' upward to new farms by a formula usually governed by office longevity and production history. As vacancies are filled higher in the chain, lower slots become available. A few occurrences normal to day-to-day real estate can occasionally generate some hard feelings in an otherwise well-managed farm system. The most frequent and hardest to deal with are incursions by fellow agents into a farm, justified by an invitation to list coming from a seller met or known by the agent outside of any geographical context. Another gray area in many new farmers' minds is what happens to ''cold calls'' coming to an office and taken by the agent-on-floor, with requests for listing information. Does the floor agent take the call, possibly an entrée to a listing, or does that agent have the duty to hand the call off to the farmer handling that part of town? (Note: We're not offering yea, nay or a solution to the above two situations—just posing questions for you to ask a broker during an affiliation interview.)

Here's a quickie question that we won't even try to find an answer to—just food for thought: Should an agent farm his or her own neighborhood? The pluses are that you're there all the time, you know many residents, you know the area and schools and you have a personal interest in the neighborhood—a requisite of a good agent. Now, a minus or two: A neighbor may list with another office. You see him every night or weekend, and hopefully you can sort out the personal relationship of being golfing buddies from the business emotion caused by losing a listing.

But whether you farm your own neighborhood or another, you can look forward to this annoyance: You depart the shower to answer a doorbell and find yourself face to face with a competing real estate agent offering a free market analysis or a stir-fry recipe. Be nice, we're all in this business together.

Final note somewhat aligned to the above: In mass marketing onslaughts of an entire neighborhood or ZIP code, it's best to put a short disclaimer alluding to the fact that if a recipient of a flier or brochure is already working with another agent, that ''*this solicitation is not intended to interfere with the agency of any other licensee*'' or words to that effect. Some prudish folks among us take blind solicitations more seriously than most of us and fail to realize that we're not knowingly courting their prospects.

*   *   *   *

A few paragraphs ago, we mentioned that many agents conduct their farms with another, but we deferred to a solo act to make the words flow easier. Now we'll return to the plural: Yes, farming is made easier if two can play. The rewards are cut in half, monetarily, but free time, one of our larger rewards, is enhanced. "Team farming" is a viable concept and practiced by many agents.

When a successful area is developed by an agent in one office, it might be difficult to leave that office, associate with another and keep active in the same area, if that area is assigned already in the new office to an agent doing a credible job of servicing it. While a very few brokers or managers might forsake the current agent and reassign an established farm to accommodate a transferring agent with a dynamite clientele, don't depend on that happening often. Dynamite producers write their own ticket when they elect to change offices, but a manager redistricting farms to accommodate them, now that would bother everyone in the inbound office, directly involved or not. We have it on good authority that Hatfield had a great farm going until she left McCoy Realty with her client file.

*   *   *   *

An entire volume could no doubt be devoted to the non-agricultural venture known in our business as "the farm," and indeed it probably has already been written, so we're not out to explore every element of the practice on a nationwide basis. We are, however, trying to create a fount of information for Future Farmers of America about the practice so that they may ask all the right questions of the brokerage office managers they speak with prior to associating with a new firm. The farm plays a large part in business acquisition in many offices and locales. In other markets, where farming is of less importance, it's treated casually—a stepchild to other, more productive endeavors. The key questions are whether the farm system is practiced and seems to be integral to success, and how soon a new agent might expect to be assigned to his or her own farm. Other related topics include "moving up" in the area assignment ladder and, finally, the stability and permanence of the typical office farmer with respect to intraoffice and new-agent dilution of an assigned farm.

And one question in closing: Does the office boast at least one secretary who occasionally tells a phone caller that "so-and-so is out in 'her farm'"? That revelation, conveyed by most offices' receptionists every so often, carries a money-back guarantee to stir up a prospect's curiosity.

From Here to Affinity

Many times we've heard an agent paraphrase this thought: "I'd rather farm a *group* than a neighborhood."

The implication is that they'd rather form a business affinity with a group of people brought together by a common thread of employment, leisure activity or political or civic involvement than a group defined by a neighborhood. The people within that affinity group form the nucleus of that agent's farm and may expect soon to come to know in no uncertain terms that the new member of the group is a real estate agent.

We'll lay a thought on the line: Veteran agents agree that the affinity farm is likely to be the vehicle that brings their careers to fruition. The neighborhood-based farm is great to get a new agent going and to generate a healthy income during the early career years when youth, stamina and dedication persist. But the affinity farm seems to be what most vets adapt to, consciously or otherwise. We'll talk more of that soon, but first, a little housekeeping.

Several cautions are appropriate for the young licensee considering this "affinity" farm. An initial caution is that in a neighborhood farm the agent is known to be exactly that, and he visits the neighborhood with the obvious intent of pursuing a business endeavor. Success will be governed by whatever factors and considerations induce or deny success, but no one can say that he entered the neighborhood on a social pretense for business purposes.

Alas, some real estate agents who join an affinity group with the tacit underlying intent of furthering a brokerage career eventually and usually will provoke such an accusation. (Somewhat less irritating, but not by much, is the non-licensed, long-standing member of such a group who attains a license.) He or she comes into the group as a soprano or a shortstop, a docent or a dancer, but in time will be exposed as a Trojan Horse, using the group's time and resources for personal gain.

*   *   *   *

In recent times, resistance has been running high against conversion of social and quasi-business associations into farm areas not only for real estate agents but for many other salespeople, and these clubs have become less fertile fields for a contact-happy agent to plow. We know of clubs and groups that use only home addresses and telephone numbers in the group roster and others that dispatch the sergeant-at-arms with a mug to collect fairly heavy-duty fines for commercializing the proceedings. About eight bars of a commercial pitch at our barbershop chorus meeting will send an off-key crooner packing.

The message is that if you like to sing bass, cook chili, hang glide, play bridge, volunteer at a hospital or do about any other all-American activity that usually can be found in the charter of a local club or association, then do so, but don't spend good money on dues just to learn that "Mama don't allow no real estate farming 'round here."

(And if Mama does allow it, about half of your local competitors have probably joined by now.)

* * * *

A lamentable eventuality of outlawing real estate patter at the weekly meeting of the Downtown Strutters' Chowder and Marching Society is that all that's left to do at the meeting is eat chowder or march, which is supposed to be why you joined in the first place. That thought forms the basis of the Affinity Farm segment of this chapter: Do what you enjoy doing as an individual, not as a licensee, in your leisure hours, and you'll probably do about as much business with your group as you are destined to do. You'll be more relaxed, and your friends in the club will definitely be more comfortable.

Frankly, "farming" is almost a misnomer when coupled with "affinity." Farming implies an open and overt effort to make contacts and preserve a presence with a group of potential clients while our greatest successes with an affinity group usually occur in an atmosphere of subtlety.

A few paragraphs ago we indicated that the affinity farm held more promise as a long-haul *modus operandi* for maturing agents due to a lesser demand for the unrelenting effort required in neighborhood farming. A look around your town at successful agents will usually reveal that the people who get out and about are usually the busiest. The groups, or affinities, they join vary widely, but be assured that the agents are probably a bit low-key about their profession and that a non-threatening, non-soliciting attitude put them at the top of the local ladder.

And at some point in a vet's career, the affinity group, the chorus or the bridge club, loses identity as the agent's farm; with experience and exposure, and a popular and ethical track record, the whole world becomes that licensee's oyster.

The Contact Within

Departing from the types of business bases addressed thus far and known in most parts of the country as "farms"—neighborhood and affinity—several other definable ways to root out new clients work well for many of us.

An initial tactic might come too late in these pages for some of us: An aspiring real estate broker courts a suitable friend as early as the third or fourth grade, trains him or her well, eventually marries and covertly dispatches this disciplined spouse into the personnel office of a great telephone company about to suffer divestiture.

The above words are a bit fanciful but convey the secret of success of many agents—a well-placed friend or spouse can do wonders for business. In a world recently traumatized by insider information-type abuses in industry, rest assured that we're "agin'" it, and we're not supporting or endorsing an illegal act. The simple advice is, if you have an ethical ace, play it, so long as all involved parties are winners and the competition comes out no less than even.

An important note here is compensation and finder's fees. In our state, and probably yours, payment of part of a commission as compensation to a non-licensee is illegal. Should a tip result in a sales opportunity, a nice dinner is fine and, better yet, legal. To keep the last few paragraphs in perspective, we're not really anticipating that you're about to break into the war room of Ma Bell or Big Blue. What we're really visualizing is an occasional transaction arising from an ear-to-the-ground contact within a modest-size local firm.

Chain Reactions

The fourth and final segment in our enumeration of marketing categories that produce a sum greater than the parts is the cultivation of clients who have coworkers following them to your town, all of whom need roofs over their heads. Infrequently, what seems a chance encounter with a lone prospect may be only the tip of an iceberg. Witness two examples that were probably echoed all over the country in the mid-eighties: The airline with the smile and the manufacturer of a demure compact car both decided to make a significant personnel commitment to our town. Translated, the centralized ticketing facility of PSA (Pacific Southwest Airlines) and the North American headquarters of Porsche relocated to Reno.

Many a real estate agent who had a pleasant and successful transaction with one of these inbound corporate transferees was pleased to learn that their newfound clients had a number of coworkers following them up the San Diego Freeway, and for some agents, one sale led to another, and another.

The message: Keep your horizons open and hearken to the agent/host/travel-guide language in a later chapter. The suggestion: Ask corporate clients point-blank if other coworkers are destined for your town, and create an early alliance with any who have even a casual inquiry about your area.

*   *   *   *

We'll review the four concepts contained thus far in the text, then move on into some less defined areas of business development.

The first category: Neighborhood farming. The prospects are all holding still, like ducks frozen on a pond, and we go out and meet them and build a relationship. The second category: Affinity groups—the ducks scatter but regroup every now and then, and we're there in the flock, building and maintaining our relationship. Note the warning in the text: We meet for all the right reasons first, and if some business results, great, but we're not disappointed if all the meeting promises is just an evening with friends.

A third category of business comes from friends in the right places whom we've trusted to keep an ear to the ground for new business. Some would call this farming, as in a business office variation of the neighborhood farm, but recognize the difference: In a neighborhood farm the agent meets the residents face-to-face and builds a relationship. In this third variation the client may only be known to the agent as the person who's been transferred in from the St. Paul office and needs a home for his or her family.

And the final category in this group, the chain reaction, where dumb luck and clean living result in a person visiting your office who not only needs a home herself but is on the advance team scouting out housing for a dozen more coworkers. And another note is appropriate here—many corporate transferees come to town unfettered by the necessity of selling the old family manse in their former town. Corporate relocation is Big Business, and many companies have recognized the need to buy or to market or at least to compensate the outbound employee for the real estate commission and cost of selling their existing home.

Having one such person across your desk or in your minivan, with a procession of his or her friends *en route* is the stuff of dreams to a real estate person.

*   *   *   *

In all the text thus far, one common thread has been drawn: Activity within each of the four categories by a licensee usually results in exposure, contact or an enhanced relationship with more than one prospect at a time—more bang for the buck, as a Pentagon hawk might say.

For that reason, we've devoted a fair amount of ink to each topic. The message to a first-year agent is that whatever other activities you conduct in marketing yourself and your office, keep the multiple-contact theory in the back of your mind and maximize the impact of your efforts.

The "Relo" Program

A comment taken from a few paragraphs ago leads off the relocation program text—think back to the chatter about an employee relocating to your town and telling ten friends about the great real estate agent who found their new home.

As a practical matter, the ten friends, if they are to gain the benefit of their company's transfer package that includes picking up commissions and other costs of selling their home, may be asked to list with a certain agent in the town they are leaving. And (/or) they may be required to register with a relocation company, which will place their name in a pool to be sent along to agents in the destination city.

A look at the process: The real estate firm in the originating city transmits the name of the corporate client's transferred employee to the national or regional headquarters of a relocation company. This company may be owned by or aligned with one major real estate franchise, or it may be a nationwide company that franchises the right to access its client file to a number of other franchised firms. Restated, some major brokerage franchises have an internal relo arm, others subscribe to a service. Listing with one franchise when leaving Ohio does not necessarily imply working with the same franchise upon arriving in Arizona.

The relo company, upon receiving the employee's name, transmits the name to the member office in the destination city. That office, upon receiving the name, assigns it out to the next agent in the rotation, who makes contact with the employee and arranges for advance information to be mailed and showing appointments upon the employee's arrival in town. The relo company keeps track of the progress of the transaction.

From the transferee's standpoint, it's a comfortable way of doing business. Picking a real estate agent in a strange town is tough while arriving in town with an agent's name in hand, no doubt with the beginning of a relationship already formed through a few telephone conversations, is a great ice-breaker. And the transferee-buyer's confidence in the agent is enhanced by the fact that he or she was recommended by a major relocation agency. Those agencies look out for the interests of their client's employees diligently—a house-hunting, lower-management cog in the corporate wheel personifies Standard Oil or McDonnell Douglas for a week or two and should be treated like royalty.

*   *   *   *

It's a good system, at least as good as the people on both ends of the string, with the company in the middle. It generates in most cases for-real and qualified prospects, and you'd be well advised to get into the relo pool in your office.

A few thoughts are appropriate, and here we'll really yield in advance to local case practice. Number one, the employee may or may not be free to work with any agent she chooses in the destination city, in spite of coming to town to meet one assigned agent. Many swords have been rattled over this point, and virtual "ownership" of the employee has been asserted, but she can do business with whomever she chooses if the assigned agent doesn't measure up to what she has in mind.

Another point is that the relocation companies do not do this as a public service and out of the goodness of their corporate hearts. You may expect a part of your commission, if the tip pays off, to be directed in escrow to "relocation."

The Relocation Listing

Obviously, when the employee vacates the family home, something has to happen to it too, and the relo company kindly offers to take it on as a project.

In a manner similar to the destination city pool and rotation, the vacated home is assigned to a local office, which then assigns it to an agent to market and sell. An appraisal is usually made to determine price, and relo, while seldom holding actual title to the home, acts as the seller. (The transferred employee occasionally executes a deed with a blank grantee and/or a power of attorney to the relocation company. The company generally executes a listing.)

The bulk of text regarding treatment of such a home is contained in a later chapter about vacated listings. For the purpose of this chapter, suffice it to say that this category of business is significant and valuable to a new agent who can get aboard an office relocation program.

*   *   *   *

Some brokerage offices regard a slot in the relocation rotation as a privilege to be earned, thus it is not always a business-generation tool available to the newcomer. Like many other areas explored in this chapter, we're not trying to cover a topic to its maximum scope but rather trying to get all the pertinent questions out on the table. The question of access to relocation business, and at what stage of your career, is a very incisive one to settle with your broker.

Employee relocation in today's mobile America is a major source of business for our industry and many ancillary industries. The relocation companies perform a vital service to both the employer, who is virtually obligated to take on the responsibility of the employee's present home, and to the employee, who already has enough to think about during the major upheaval in their lives that an intercity move generates. No one loses—the relo company, the brokerage firm(s), agents in two different towns and the employee come out ahead during a well-orchestrated sale and purchase.

Don't rely on only our text for information—relocation on a nationwide basis is a complicated and varying service, and we're purposely skirting any specifics. But business it is, and good business at that. When you next seek a firm to associate with, their relocation program might form an interesting segment of your interview.

And if they don't subscribe to a relo, don't be put off. Many relocating employees just pick up a local real estate weekly guide at the airport, so you're still in the running!

Read Between the Lines

From here, you're pretty much on your own—we've popped up four categories of multiple-prospect contacting that have worked well for many of us and might form a foundation for newer agents. The relocation companies are fairly well established as an integral influence upon real estate brokerage. With luck, you'll work as a relo lister with a wide-eyed, first-time visitor/buyer early in your career.

We won't write of the many contacts you're likely to make in the years in real estate that lie in front of you—time doesn't permit, they're too varied and you wouldn't believe them anyway. But you will look back in awe a decade from now at some situations you encountered and know then why we didn't even try to tackle them in a book.

The thrusts of this chapter were the four multiple-prospect activities of "farming" and the benefits of relocation, both in listing and selling. These elements of our business usually form the basis of later success.

We will throw down a challenge for you to convert into a habit, a game you can play every time you pick up a newspaper or take a ride through town. The challenge is to see a news story, an ad, a doughnut shop opening or a bank being bought out and foresee the real estate opportunities the act represents. Baseball fans portended the end of an era when Reggie left the As to be a Yankee—disciplined real estate people saw only a listing in Oakland and a sale in New York. Nothing less, nothing more; seeking business becomes instinctive.

*   *   *   *

Ask your coworkers and you'll find that no person or situation is outside the bounds of a workable deal. Some are just stranger than others. We like personal examples and started to close the chapter with a favorite, involving our Harley Davidson, a vacant lot and a Maryknoll nun in an Austin Healy but realized that nobody'd believe it anyway.

We did sell the lot (to her brother!).

For the Record

An influential executive somewhere on the Eastern Seaboard once employed the definitive recordkeeping system: A tape recorder started before the boss arrived at the store. The thing ran all day, picking up everything that transpired in the office.

But a glitch developed when a secretary accidentally backed into the wrong button on the recording equipment, excising 43 minutes from the executive's day and creating for him no end of inconvenience.

All that's too sophisticated for us—we'll just stick with our backwoods steno pads.

* * * *

We have a friend in real estate known for his propensity for recordkeeping. Scarcely a casual comment or the ring of a phone fails to result in a glance at his wristwatch, the tug of a pen from his pocket and a scribble into a well-worn leather notebook that he's been packing around for two decades and constantly refilling with fresh pads of paper. His antics have become legion to the extent that he is regarded as the local archivist of the industry.

A few of his closer friends know that the man is probably the worst recordkeeper ever to walk the face of the earth. Owing to his illegible penmanship, disorganized notes and total inability to locate the pad of filler paper last used in his notebook, we're surprised he can find his car in the parking lot after a ball game.

But to the amusement of all of us who know this little secret, no outsiders will dispute his word. If he says the pest control report was ordered on March 17th, that's when it was ordered; the date's bound to be in the book. (It's not, but the ruse works, and the inexperienced leave him unchallenged.)

The "in" group anxiously await the day he gets subpoenaed to a trial as a witness and has to display his Hefty bag full of graffiti under oath—we'll all be in the gallery.

Four Basic Systems

We'll look at several methods of organizing the facts that experienced real estate agents usually retain. Whether they view them as analytically as we will now is doubtful—most of us enter the business and our records system just grows, like Topsy. The four base systems are: 1) a daily log of our activities; 2) facts organized geographically, e.g., by street addresses of properties; 3) facts about people; and 4) financial records. You will no doubt change or embellish these categories and combine or merge them into a comfortable method of doing the job, but do it. What we all need is the "D" word: Discipline.

*   *   *   *

A Daily Record.   From the top with category number one: You've probably been keeping such records since fifth grade when you wrote "Dear Diary" about the hunk in P.E. class that you'd like to take home to Mother when Mother wasn't home. That depth of detail is what we're advocating here—not just what you did but what time and where you were when you did it, who else was there and an encapsulation of the meeting or occasion. A cryptic "Joe C." penciled after the 2:00 P.M. blank in your Day-Timer may not mean much six months later, but the enhanced entry could pull you through a tight spot.

All that effort relates to the past tense; now, we'll use the same format to log our commitments for the future. Nothing magic here—just an appointment book. Note down "Joe C." a week before the meeting, then follow up with the full story when the appointment's over.

In the next to last paragraph we mentioned the Day-Timer, and while we're not large on making product endorsements, the Day-Timer system has worked well for many agents. They're available in twelve-month sets, handy for setting appointments several months in advance, but only the current month need be hauled around on a daily basis. The rest of the year resides in a nice plastic case delivered with the set. A side benefit is that you can buy a set starting with any month of the year; few business necessities chafe more than having to buy a calendar in October!

Real estate agents keep daily appointment books somewhat differently from a truly normal person. The normals have a desktop appointment book at the office for meetings with "Joe C." and a calendar by the telephone in the kitchen at home for bridge games and Little League practice. Not so for real estate types, who frequently switch the normals' schedules upside down by golfing in the morning and showing homes at night. Buy one book for your business *and* leisure activities, memorialize your whole life within its pages and you'll never schedule a tee time simultaneously with a showing appointment. Well, almost never.

*   *   *   *

Street Addresses.   Next item of business is a file of street addresses. Please take note that no further qualifiers have been used—just street addresses, any address that for some reason is interesting to you. You don't have to have it listed for sale or have sold it, nor does the address have to be a home that's on the market. If for some reason it piques your fancy, you track it.

A suggested format is a set of cards, maybe 3x5″, in a steel file box, arranged alphabetically by street and ascending street number. Such cards are available to real estate people in our trade magazines from a number of printers, and most variations have a great many blanks for information, such as owner, tax parcel, room-by-room description, lot size—usually more information than can ever be squeezed into the MLS books.

The obvious use is for a home you're listing, or trying to list, or a home you've sold. But expand the file from there. We've shown homes to prospects and failed to sell the homes, but were impressed enough with the homes to make cards for them. Years later, when the homes again went on the market, we had a great memory-jogger right in our own office, in more depth than the information in the MLS. You'll be in business for many years, and if you're like many of us, you'll probably tend to concentrate your expertise in one area of town. Most veterans agree that there's a certain comfort zone in becoming the resident expert in an area and then staying on your own turf.

Work your card system—it's a resource free for the asking. If a home makes the news, make a card for it. A home on our turf went on the market a few years ago, and the address rang a bell. Actually it rang a four-alarm gong—we had an ancient card on file, with the notation that the roof burned off from a lightning strike a decade before. The value? Negligible, unless we sold the home. We'd rather such a little tidbit come from us as a broker than from a neighbor after the buyers move in.

*   *   *   *

People.   Now, a file on humans—like the address cards above, no further qualifiers—just humans with whom your business brings you into contact. We'll offer an example of the benefit of such a file:

You're on floor time, and Mr. X calls about an ad. While you're talking, your fingers are flying through the Rolodex, and you find that a person with the same name visited an open house several months ago. "Are you the Mr. X who has three kids and needs to be close to a pizza parlor?" The file card has enabled you to rekindle a business relationship. And put yourself in his place—isn't it nice when a merchant remembers your name?

During our early years in residential brokerage, we hit biographical records hard, creating cards for people as we met them. Then we updated the cards to reflect married names, employers, babies as they arrived, birth dates and anything else about people that could be useful in maintaining client relationships. Obviously, as they entered the hallowed status of becoming a home purchaser or seller, we cross-referenced their names to the other party's and the property address.

The cards were a lot of work, but with experience we found that we could do them in our sleep. We don't regret a minute of it—they did their job. And never throw out a card—if it fills up, start another one. If Ralph marries Alice, leave Alice's card intact and cross-reference it to a new one for Ralph. A year from now when you can't remember Ralph's last name, Alice's card will refresh your memory. Was it *Kramden?*

*   *   *   *

Financial Records.   We identify financial records as a separate category of files to maintain in order to establish that category as a crucial duty in real estate brokerage. In truth, financial records are a logical adjunct to our first category, the daily log of activities. The best time to scratch down into Dear Diary the fact that you bought a tank of gas is right while you're paying for it. And don't stop there—write down the mileage and which car the fuel went into if you use a second car occasionally.

The records are kept for the benefit of many, or restated for your benefit at the insistence of many. High on our list, possibly yours also, is an Uncle named Sam, who occasionally inquires as to how we managed to put 27,431 miles on our GMC Suburban in an effort to sell four homes, or how we consumed 42 bottles of White-Out in writing a 212-page manuscript. You may have a similar family member, and you'll find that while the records you keep may be worthless in documenting such a motoring odyssey or gluttony of office supplies, they do get an audit off to a relaxed start following a little comic relief.

*   *   *   *

We believe that about the only thing more irritating than a CPA trying to sell a home is a real estate agent offering tax advice. Therefore, we'll not encroach on our accounting friends too far other than to tell you to seek the advice of an accounting pro very early in your brokerage endeavor. You'll probably learn that the existence of expense records will have a significant impact on your net income throughout the successful career you've embarked upon.

Ask about entertaining: What stubs and receipts constitute acceptable records, what notations should be kept about which client/prospect and why you incurred an entertainment expense. We mentioned fuel and auto expense records and receipts. Get your accountant's opinion about apportioning usage between business and pleasure trips, and the best way to keep records of them. The term "contemporaneous record" will probably come up; it derives from the Latin "to habitually reach for a pad to write on as you buckle your seat belt," or, alternatively, "the desire to look at your odometer as you turn off your ignition key."

*   *   *   *

In plain English, keep an accurate log of your auto use, not by day or week but by trip. Record the necessity for and the distance of each definable operation of the car. The need for diligent records by real estate people is elevated by our daily schedules, which reach into evenings, our weekend business activities and a propensity to combine personal pursuits with business endeavors throughout the day as free time permits.

To the amazement of many, contemporaneous auto records become almost second nature with a little of the "D" word. Make it a habit— the last two numbers on the odometer usually suffice. Many of us use a pocket microcassette-size dictating machine, dedicated to nothing but car mileage use. They're light, cheap, work easily with one hand and stuff under the front seat between trips. Tell the tape what day it is the first thing in the morning, then tell it where you're taking it and why as you move around town, always ending the notation with odometer readings. Once or twice a week when you're *really* bored, correlate the mileage into your daily log.

Most veterans have learned that it's just easier to keep contemporaneous records than to sweat out an audit. While the history we build each year may not measure up to a NASA-tech flight tape (which, parenthetically, your 1040 and mine subsidize), our CPA friends tell us that reasonable accuracy will usually get us through the day.

Unless, of course, you document 27,431 miles while selling four homes.

Phone Bills

If you're doing a brisk enough business, you're also probably reaching out and touching someone, telephonically speaking, on a frequent enough basis to make telephone-related expenses a significant entry in your datebook. Ask your accountant about two categories of phone expenses:

The most obvious are toll-related charges—message units for time and distance across the county and even more significant long-distance calls (although many intrastate calls are costlier than others across half a continent!). And don't forget the inbound toll calls generated by inviting a traveling client or prospect residing outside of state to call you collect. Occasionally in this modernized age some of us forget why the FAX machine exists, and we send a Western Union telegram or Mailgram. This whole paragraph entreats us to methods of running up a telephone bill, and every time such a charge appears on our home statement, on our office's or on another party's statement, an entry should appear in our datebook explaining the reason for the call.

A second category of phone bills: While you're talking to your accountant about phones vis-à-vis your business, seek some guidance about the taxable impact of one-time telephone-related expenses—line origination and installation charges, acquisition of phones, answering machines, car phones, pagers and possibly even a FAX machine, which some agents now have in their own homes. Also ask about apportioning a home (personal) phone basic rate between business and personal use.

*   *   *   *

By adding the frequently occurring expense notations of auto mileage and fuel cost, telephone bills and entertainment outlays to the chronological history of our travels about the countryside, we start to create one fat little datebook. But don't stop with the above categories of expenses—the book's a good place to record almost any expense you incur on a business basis, whether making a duplicate key or buying a Polaroid camera. It may not be the ultimate archive, but it's the one in your pocket that will remind you to enter the expense in a more complete journal later.

The necessity of retaining receipts and sales slips shouldn't need a separate chapter. If you part with even one thin dime in the furtherance of a client's interest, get a receipt and file it in some consistent fashion. It may be by client, by home, by month, by expense category (e.g., keys, cameras, real estate books) or by any other system that works for you, but file it you should.

Office Records

Throughout the chapter thus far, we've used the words *should* and *agent*. Now we'll shift to *must* and *office* because the next type of record is basically non-negotiable in the eyes of most state regulatory bodies. These are the transaction files, containing a complete history of the conveyance of a property from the moment of listing through the day escrow closes, and conceivably any events pertaining to the conveyance that occurred following the closing.

State regulatory agencies look to the broker of record to compile and retain these records, but be assured that your broker will look to Guess-Who to help out, so we'll talk in the context of *you* maintaining the files on properties you list or sell. And a point should be made about which of these activities dictates the file maintenance: Listings resulting in a sale or listings with no conveyance resulting. The other side of that coin: Rejected or expired offers. Most veterans have a monster file of those unsuccessful offers—they're not orderly or pretty, but it beats throwing away a record that could be significant in the future.

At the risk of getting a letter or two from a state bureau to clarify their interpretation of our obligation, we'll offer the thought that one duty of the collective state bureaus is to protect the public. If our office were ever in the position of having to answer to the State of Nevada R.E.D. about an advertisement or other vehicle we used to motivate a buyer, it would be mighty nice to have a file on every listing, whether or not it went to a conveyance. For this reason, most well-run offices maintain files on *all* listings, sold or not, and we're told that most states prefer this as a standard of practice. The message: Even if your listing runs out and reappears through an agent across town, commit your file to the statutory length of permanence, seven years in our state.

*   *   *   *

Which brings up an interesting point: Who is entitled to view the files? Our state agencies are certainly entitled to have them retrieved from some dusty basement, and the parties to the transaction should have the right to see them. But other parties occasionally come forth with a reason to review records that on the surface appears logical but might not be legitimate. Bear in mind that your fiduciary obligation to the client and other parties to the transaction does not cease on the day that escrow closed—you are still bound by confidentiality. When receiving requests for files, we usually tell the party to request the file from our principals; then we assure them that we will locate the file upon our principals' request.

What we're advocating in the recordkeeping department is to start a file in a manila folder on the day that the reasonable probability of completing a transaction occurs. Events, statements and representations leading to a listing are germane to the transaction even prior to the signed listing. Similarly, contacts with buyers should be recorded when the tone gets serious. From that date forward, any activity should be entered as a longhand notation on the folder or by inclusion of a document within it. At close of escrow, the closing agent's statement together with commission settlements will complete the file. Subsequent correspondence with the parties should also find its way into the file.

Personal Files

The above activity is dictated by state statute. Sure, it's for convenience while you're marketing and closing the sale. But at conveyance, the file has done its job and usually goes down to the basement with your office's other transaction files. Or it can be microfiched and indexed.

And you may never see it again. More probably, you could retrieve it, but that might be a little tougher after it leaves the "active" file rack on your desk.

So we'll advocate one final type of record in this chapter: A recreation of the transaction file, which will remain within your custody—a gleaning of anything in the file that can help you keep in touch with buyers and sellers. We're departing from statutory recordkeeping now and returning to a marketing context. Maintenance of client relationships is the name of that tune, and you will certainly be presented with the opportunity some day to list a home that you sold earlier in your career. Climbing around the basement looking for the old file is cumbersome; what's worse is returning hat-in-hand to your old office for the file, in the event that you have changed affiliations during the intervening period.

Make it easy on yourself while the timing's right—keep a photo-copy of the more important elements of the transaction file. (You'll need far less than the full, permanent broker version.) Keep them in your possession, and consider this final tip: Buy some small cards, business-card size is fine, in three different colors. Now cross-reference buyers, sellers, and addresses, with each category alphabet-ized on a different color card. You may not believe it at this juncture of your career, but you can start looking forward to the day when you know you sold somebody's home but can't remember where it was or who bought it. When you arrive at that stage of disoriented fuzziness, you'll know that you're finally well along the path to success in real estate!

And, of Course, the Computer

On the way now to a chapter about floor calls, we'll admit that we overheard a reader ask why a PC wouldn't be a boon to recordkeeping. Some would say that computer talk should have been paramount in this chapter, and they may be right.

In analyzing most of our needs, we couldn't endorse their use in more glowing terms. Most veterans would love to toss out shoebox af-ter shoebox full of yellowing pads, but we don't have the heart to do it because about once a year a note in our shoebox saves our hide. How nice it would be now to have started a hard disk full of prospects many years ago, to have updated it and now be able to pull up a Holiday card list. Alas, the only computers in our town then made the street lights go dim when they were ''booted up'' each morning.

The goals of this chapter haven't been changed by the technology—the only change is the time reduction in storing and re-trieving information. If you have a PC, you should definitely consider recording some activities of your daily real estate pursuits. Software written for real estate agents' needs is available through ads in most of our trade magazines. But don't totally forsake the spiral notebook in your purse or the Ticonderoga #2 behind your ear. Real estate people do a *lot* of business far away from 110-volt power!

6

Floorgone Conclusions

A receptionist sounded the universal battle cry of the American real estate office: "Who's on Floor?" The assembled sales staff, in one robust voice that would have made Gilbert and Sullivan proud, declared "'Tis I!"

As the salaried staff took cover, the assembled neophytes, two dozen strong, juggled the dog-eared floor book around the room like a jump ball over the parquet of Boston Gardens until a dainty saleslady rebounded it, dribbled it to her desk and took the prospect's call, Bird-like, of course.

* * * *

We were visiting the office, merely dropping off a key, when this carnage erupted. As we crouched under a conference table with several paid staffers, we asked the receptionist if telephone coverage was always this hearty, wondering if we could instill the same feeding-frenzy enthusiasm in our own office staff if it ever grew larger than two people.

"This is Saturday morning," she allowed. "Try to get even one of them to take a call at four o'clock on a Thursday."

* * * *

"Floor time" is the stuff of this chapter, a mainstay of residential brokerage also known as "opportunity time," or just "op time" in some offices. There are probably as many variations of floor time administration as there are real estate offices. The thoughts that follow in the next few pages are usually incorporated, albeit somewhat clouded over, in most of those offices. We'll be very honest on another score: This book is not destined to go into competition with the many excellent magazine articles, books and audio/video tapes that reveal what to say to a prospect while fielding a floor call. We like those resources, but prospects and agents vary enormously, and we'd like to finish this chapter while we're still in our forties.

Finally, it should be noted as we get underway that a fair number of offices are opting for a computer-supported floor/inventory system. Such technology, wisely used by the human at the keyboard, places those offices light years ahead of the majority using the manual, loose-leaf page system prevalent in our industry. (Which is not to say that a well-trained staff using a manual system and pulling in unison can't be competitive with a disk-supported office.)

We'll give a byte of attention to the lucky minority with PCs, but the main thrust of this chapter is more in tune with the goal of a strong floor system than the devices we use to achieve that goal.

The People

A universal concern to newer agents is the amount of floor time they will be able to cover. An analytical thinker arriving at a new office might count the licenses on the office's wall and divide them by the number of floor shifts in a day—usually two or three. Three shifts, 27 licenses, let's see: That's floor time every ninth day. Three a month—pretty thin.

Now, talk to a few of your associates or to your manager and find out what really happens: Of the 27 agents in the office, a number of them, and usually a substantial number, think home buyers were put on earth only to drive real estate agents crazy, and they simply refuse to take floor time. "Listers," after several years in the business, only list homes, and you're welcome to their floor time. (Office managers are paid to declare on an annual basis that every agent in the office *will* take floor time *or else.* The lady who listed three mil last year then quietly inquires, "Or else what?" and the floor-rotation issue quiets right down.)

So our 27 agents are now, say, 18—since 9 want nothing to do with buyers, ever. Of the 18 agents, 4 might be out of town in any given week, and 14 agents divided by 3 slots a day starts to look like steady work.

Now, we get predatory: Agents who actually *like* floor time can hover around the office waiting for an agent to give up assigned time in favor of a last-minute diversion such as an out-of-town client, an appointment running late or White Flower Days at Macy's.

Our imaginary 27-agent office with 3 daily floor times promised a shift only every 9 days. In reality, whether the office has 10, 27 or 90 agents, working 2, 3 or 4 daily shifts (some offices remain open until well into the evening), with 1 or 2 agents on floor at once, newcomers who are real hustlers can probably get a lot more floor time than the mathematical equation promises, usually quite early in their careers.

*   *   *   *

Now, some housekeeping about the preceding text: Many offices have policies about changing floor time once agents have their assignments on a schedule. Some managers prefer that the time slot you might abdicate be reassigned on a "waiting list" basis to agents who have requested additional time—that the time not be taken by an agent orbiting vulture-like around the office in hopes of pouncing on unattended prospect calls.

As a former manager of a 22-agent office (for one very long year), we would have been pleased and proud to have had a baboon assist the prospect if the monkey held a license from the State of Nevada. We had things to worry about other than who was covering whose time, and we trusted the phone capabilities of all the agents in the office, *homo sapiens* or semi-simian.

But, in defense of managers who Want To Know, there is occasional abuse or ugly favoritism by floor-schedule traders. From time to time, management needs the means to steer the ship and head off possible mutinies. For that reason, what may seem picky-picky in your office may be a sound management policy if reasonably administered.

*   *   *   *

Hand-in-hand with the policies of trading or picking up floor time from scheduled agents with hot buyers, is the need for discussion with your manager early-on about office policy regarding division of compensation for calls taken during the time yielded by the other agent. The simple fact is that you take her time speculatively while she leaves with the anticipation of making a commission.

Unpleasant discussions often arise if you receive a solid-gold call during her floor time and make a sale. And the tenor of the discussion really heats up if the appointment for which she ceded her floor time results in a goose egg.

A sharp manager will have a policy about this eventuality—it's one that happens all too often. Like many aspects of working with people, you'll find that small groups of individuals within the office are quite comfortable with inside arrangements to cover these matters. But you, if you're a new person, have a right to an understanding of your compensation in advance. Ask your manager early in your association about intraoffice commission division prior to paving a path to disappointment or contention with your coworkers.

The Floor Book

We've read of an automated real estate floor program that must have been invented by the same charmer that gave the phone companies the Information system: If an operator can say "Hello, what city and name?" then he or she can make a living by keystroking your answer and letting you hear the computer's voice-synthesized response provide your party's phone listing.

The real estate application goes about the same way. An interested buyer gives a code number on a yard sign or a newspaper ad to a human agent, who enters the number on a keyboard and lets the buyer hear a glowing, professionally prerecorded account of the home.

In the real world, however, a real estate agent takes a call from a prospect and deals with it through training, experience, a certain fleetness of fact and a snippet of stealth. She is, in a word, a pro.

*   *   *   *

A vast number of offices in our nation still use a floor book, a binder, if you will, or a card flip-file or a variation of both—in effect, a portable encapsulation of the office's listing inventory bound in a color unlike any other binder found in the office. Some are treated to induce a myocardial infarction if anyone dares carry the book away from the office. But some offices do maintain a "traveling floor book," nice to have when the weather or a holiday render weekend time spent at the office next to useless, yet you still wish to muster some semblance of responsiveness when call-forwarding brings a call to your home. However, most managers agree that the tools of the trade, listing keys, the copy machine and all the rest of what we need remain at the office, and floor time should best be taken there, not at home.

Before we open that floor book, let's think about the function it serves: It's the Express Lane, eight-items-or-less, cash-only checkstand through the office's inventory for the agent "on-floor," who statistically has less than a minute to match information with a caller's request or risk losing credibility with that caller. We don't need pretty here; pretty can stay in the office file and the agent's backup file, neatly done while the preparer has all the time in the world.

What we want in our floor book is true jungle real estate—big bold index letters under glassine holders, enabling quick location of a listing in about five flips, usually keyed around one of three denominators, which follow soon.

Picture yourself as the prospect interested in a home: You saw a sign on a home, maybe you can remember the street and then again maybe not, but you know it was in a certain part of town. Or it was in the paper, unclear as to address, but advertised at $200,000.

*   *   *   *

A sharp floor agent should be able to find that home in her office's book with any one of three denominators: Easiest is the "address," but don't depend on buyers who have looked at yard signs all weekend to come up with the correct street name. In our own town and neighboring Sparks, we had at last count no less than 54 streets rooted in variants of the word Spring. Agents who live here, let alone out-of-town buyers in a Hertz sedan, can't keep them all straight.

If you do get a street address, you've usually got it made. Denominator II is prevalent: The buyers recall a "geographical area," which is frequently the primary organizational "family" in many office floor books, and within that family listings are frequently arranged in ascending listing price. Most buyers, even the terminally disoriented, are reasonably clear on at least the area of town or residential district they visited and can be zeroed in by the description of the home.

The third primary denominator for organizing a floor system is alluded to above: The "asking price." This root favors an advertisement-oriented rather than a yard-sign-oriented office.

*   *   *   *

We made short shrift of the street-address list as the primary basis for organizing a floor book. You'll find that most offices just put a type-written address list in their book, referencing the agent to an area or an asking price.

The pros and cons of the remaining two roots are evident. Much of the choice between a geographical base and an asking price base is determined by the makeup of the market served by your office and by the market share or volume the office enjoys. If your office deals primarily in $125,000 to $150,000 homes throughout your town, an asking price base would fail to narrow down the caller's choice, but a geographical area would set a bell ringing. Beating the point to death, if you deal almost entirely in one area of town, then the asking price would be a better index for narrowing the field early in a floor call.

The Floor Book Continues

Some confusion has come to our office inventory system due to the proliferation of "planned unit developments," "clusters," "zero-lot-line" and townhouse/condominium listings. The differentiation of a decade ago between the pure, free-standing single family residence and a higher-density, frequently multiple-story condo has faded as garden style, often free-standing or zero lot-line P.U.D. (Planned Unit Development) homes acquire increasing demand and marketability.

Within the floor book context, the dilemma is where to place these listings. A "condo/P.U.D." subsection within each area or price range is tough to administer. Many offices solve the problem by widening the parameters of price and combining several areas into one larger region, thus creating a floor book section known by a number of monikers, all suggesting "density homes." Other offices, in growing numbers, seem just to ignore the type of interest the sellers hold in their property and list them in their floor books by price and area.

We'll not offer any solution, as there probably isn't one, other than consistency within your office. The objective of this text has been to offer you an insight into the complexity of the floor book system, with the hope that we've planted a few mental seeds to help you use the book to your advantage. The language thus far has been directed toward helping you locate one home out of a hundred in the floor book. In a little while, we'll discuss finding a home better suited to the phone prospect than the one she called about, providing the decision has been ethically reached that the home she called on is just not one she'll ever buy.

Statistics Can Be Fun

Most well-operated offices have a log used by each floorperson as they go through their activities. After the agent's name and date heading, managers usually look for a time of call, caller's name (good luck!) and the address of the listing. Onward to the source of the call (sign, newspaper, homes-guide-type fliers, open house) to help determine the effectiveness of recent advertising. Next, the log should record comments made by the caller, plus or minus, about the listing and notes about the caller herself: New in town, three kids, needs RV parking, whatever. Then the disposition—a showing appointment, W.C.B. (will call back) or possibly a "switch" (text to follow!).

These floor-time logs, available to all, enable the agent to correlate a history of activity on each listing: Number of calls, the opinions of prospects, negatives, plusses and any other information that might help the agent counsel the sellers on a better approach to marketing their home.

An alternative method is to attach a sheet to each listing in the book upon which the floorperson pencils in the above information. That's handy for the individual listing agent, but few managers want to go through the whole book for an update, and even fewer floor agents want to keep duplicate records.

All in all, there's a little backscratching bonus in working among a group of agents willing to make this kind of effort—the pulling together we mentioned early in the chapter.

We used to implore floor agents to *always check the floor book when responding to a prospect's or to another agent's call.* Information, and particularly showing instructions, become second nature to adept floor persons. But shoot from the hip, tell another agent to use the lockbox on the back door, and you may learn too late that the listing in the floor book had a little yellow sticker telling agents that today and tomorrow the sellers are watching their daughter-in-law's Rottweiler.

The Hot List

We all hate to admit it, but there are a few homes out there that are a bit more exciting than the others, and these are the ones likely to wind up on the sales manager's "Hot List." This list ranges from addresses on a few sheets of paper or a chalkboard in some offices and swells to a bound mini-floor book in others, and is compiled on a daily or weekly basis. The purpose of the list is twofold: To anticipate calls on certain homes and thereby speed up the agent's response, and to provide enhanced information about the homes in the floor book.

The newness of the listing is one factor here—a "For Sale" sign that went up this morning on a ho-hum house will probably produce more calls today than the sign that's been on the Taj Mahal for three months. (We tell beginning agents that the first three calls on her new listing will be from the neighbors to the left, to the right and across the street.)

Occasionally an external influence having no relationship to our listing inventory throws a little good fortune our way: Be assured that if we had a home listed on Colorado Boulevard in Pasadena we'd spend our New Year's Eve manicuring the yard before the Rose Parade passed by, and then make sure the listing information's on the Hot List.

Other candidates for the list are homes featured in the block ad we run in the Saturday morning paper that should set some bells ringing.

Now, in case one among you thinks that sales managers collect big bucks for reading *The Far Side* in their office while you're taking calls at the "Hot Desk," we'll tell you of the owner of an extremely successful office in our town a decade ago who even targeted *other office's* new listings and open houses, determined which ones were close to his office's listings and put those listings on the hot list in anticipation of increased activity. And it worked. This guy also came up with the first version that any of us in this town ever saw of the sales technique we address next: The switch list.

The Switch List

We're not going one syllable further into this tactic without a word of ethics as preface: Our fiduciary responsibility is to the seller of a home, and in the larger scheme of things, when we take a floor call about a home listed through our office, our allegiance is to the seller of *that* home even if we personally have an identical home listed a block away. We become nonseverable with the *office* as agent of the sellers, even though we may never have met them. Only after genuine diligence has been employed and a determination has been made that the home the prospects have called about is not a candidate for their needs, may we employ the techniques contained in the next few paragraphs.

And we'll share a little knowledge with you that all too many agents have learned the hard way: *Sellers delight in calling their own agent's office (or having a friend call for them) to audit the quality of representation they are receiving.* Extolling the virtue of your listing around the corner from her home, without compelling provocation (read *entrapment*) by the pseudo-prospect, could spoil your whole day.

That's a nice fact to remember when the voice on the phone seems too good to be true. It may not be.

*   *   *   *

Having mortared that ethical cornerstone into place, we'll dive headlong into the ''switch list'' for our floor book with an analogy you may find strange, but bear with us, it'll come together soon: We consider a real estate agent ''on-floor'' to be analogous to the pilot of a small airplane.

Assuming that this aviator has a well-developed sense of self-preservation, the eyes behind the goggles look for more than the Red Baron as the plane cleaves the wild blue yonder. You, in the passenger seat, see only a golf course 1,200 feet below—the experienced pilot sees 18 well-manicured and sparsely populated little runways to park upon if the rubber band breaks. It's simply instinctive, if he or she is cagey, to have a fallback alternative.

*   *   *   *

An experienced floorperson develops the same instinct. Nary a home in your inventory can be ruled out as a fallback alternative to the one your prospect has called about. Obviously, some come closer than others, and the pro learns to "switch" (ergo the technique's nickname) the prospect to another home very close in a sampling of representative categories should the initial home go sour.

When a buyer calls on one advertised home but really needs one more bedroom, can pay a little more monthly but has less to put down and would like room for an RV, the floorperson adept at switching can usually scare up two candidate homes faster than an IBM hard disk on a cold morning, and keep the conversation alive.

And it's not the gift of a savant that gives her this speed; it's hard work by a number of people: Herself, in her free time between calls; her manager, who is earning his or her keep by living up to the title of "sales manager" and devoting not a small amount of time to a switch list; and, finally, other agents, all of whom leave a few suggestions in the floor book for switches that are apparent to them. Scotch Post-It notes are dandy for leaving suggested switch listings.

Obviously, a current switch list for the entire floor book is tough to keep. It's a fluid and changing resource, as homes sell or expire and new homes come into inventory. Prioritizing is best—work up a weekly list for at least the new or "hot" listings.

*   *   *   *

Two strongly opposing schools of thought exist about the suggestion that follows. We hope you'll run it by your sales manager before you use it, and we'd be grateful if you attribute it to another real estate writer, possibly a late writer, if the manager elevates through the roof. The suggestion follows.

Don't be afraid to use a multiple listing service (other offices' inventory) as a resource to compile a switch list. Let's be honest: The time will come when your office just doesn't have the right home for a prospect or the prospect wants an amenity that's few and far between in the marketplace. If you've developed a bond with the caller and belong to an MLS system, you'd be foolish to excuse yourself from the caller with apologies and let her find the rare home through her own resources.

If your office has a home listed that's a significant departure from the mainstream of your inventory, search the other offices' listings and come up with a few alternatives to offer a caller. Half a loaf is sometimes better than none, and sometimes managers need to be told that we as an industry work for *all* sellers. If we can't help our own office's sellers and agents, let's at least help a compadre across town.

Broker Calls

As this chapter shows signs of taking on Michener-esque proportions, we advocate that you take a breather and a short walk and look forward to wrapping up the text on floor activities with some housekeeping footnotes in the few pages that follow.

Welcome back to broker calls, the bane of many floorpeople. In many offices there's not a buck to be made here—the only benefactors are the broker (usually an *agent* from another office) calling for information and the agent in your office who has the property listed. (And, of course, the seller.)

In the majority of offices that place responsibility for agent calls on the floor agent, a strong commitment to give competing agents the same cordial service we give our prospects usually results in a willingness by other offices to cobroker our listings. And a lack of this commitment over a period of time can generate a virtual *de facto* boycott of an office by other offices.

A gratis tip for agents calling another office for information: Buyer calls come first in most offices. Don't be put off if the agent-on-floor wants to call you back after she helps a prospect. Corollary tip for the floor agent: Make the appointment with the prospect, then *return the call!*

Help from a Non-Licensee

Many offices allow an unlicensed person, usually a salaried secretary or receptionist, to make showing appointments for other offices or to give out information about listed homes, primarily their availability status or showing instructions.

We've heard it said that this is illegal—that *all* representations of our listings *must* be made by licensed agents. While attending a national real estate convention, we bounced the question off a number of new friends and learned that most of them, from all over the country, shared the same impression.

After a considerable number of conversations with those who know from various ports of call around our land, we came up with a pattern that seems to be the interpretation of this notion in most areas of the country. It's a touchy issue, and we hope you'll look for local interpretation from your own state's regulatory bureau if that level of accuracy is necessary. Try this as a starter, a thought to convey to your secretary if he or she is brought into the listing information process.

It would seem that hard, verified information about a contractual listing may be disseminated by the secretary. The rub comes when the nonlicensee crosses the line from conveying only information that has been assembled by a licensee to using language *motivating* or *embellishing* the licensee's written listing information.

Therefore, "It's a three-bedroom home listed at $137,500" is OK. But, "It has a dynamite view from all three bedrooms and probably won't last at $137,500" crosses into no-no land as motivational and undocumented.

There's a Horse for Every Saddle

The home seemingly destined to spend doomsday in your floor book eventually will find a new owner. Our halftime locker-room line to sellers who swear that nobody in the world would be dumb enough to buy their home is, "You bought it, didn't you?" That always encourages them.

Purging the floor book is necessary when the status of a listed home changes. Life used to be so simple—a home was an "active" listing, in most parts of the country, and when a buyer was located, the listing went into an intermediate category. In our area we called them "pending." They were off the market, awaiting the escrow process to take them to the end of the journey to conveyance. No buyers toured them, but the sales price wasn't disclosed either. They were yanked out of the floor book as unavailable. Escrow closing was a lead-pipe cinch.

But times and the perception of our obligations have changed. The current opinion of those who gave up selling homes in order to devote full time to telling the rest of us how we should sell them is that any listing is "active" until the conveyance occurs. Restated, there is no "pending" status, *per se*, and we have an obligation to continue to market the home and to present offers to the owner so long as the home is in escrow with the initial buyers.

Interpretations of this school of thought are emerging, and if you read these words after 1990, you'd be well advised to seek an updated viewpoint. One conflict is whether we are obligated to "actively seek" offers after one has been accepted or merely to "present unsolicited" offers. And, in current thinking, a seller may release us in writing from our duty to solicit and/or present subsequent offers.

*   *   *   *

Why, you ask, is this interpretation contained in our floor-book chapter? Our response is that we need to *purify* the floor book. The question becomes: Do we pull a listing upon acceptance of an offer (creating a "pending" sale) or are we duty-bound to continue to solicit offers on the home, which we do by retaining it in our "active" inventory?

Be guided by current national and local opinion and by your office's policy as you read these words. And share the information with your sellers. Many of these folks want to know why their home is "sold" yet still being shown and in some instances advertised. (We reiterate: As this is written, the sellers can direct us to terminate marketing efforts.)

A footnote: You'll see fewer and fewer "Sold" yard sign riders in the next few years. The trend is toward "Under Contract" or "Sale Pending" in response to the preceding interpretation of our obligation.

Information Is Like Gold

We're near to closing the floor book and this chapter about it, but we'll point out one last gem before the big finish: A lot of notes went onto the listing sheet in the book—don't forsake that information. You learned of many buyers looking for a home and the type of home sought. You have phone numbers and a good relationship with those callers, and many of them still need that home.

Many real estate prospects are totally amazed that a few of us can remember their names longer than 72 hours and that we know they have 2 kids, are moving from Seattle in June and live with a mother-in-law who breeds goldfish.

Take advantage of any information garnered from your floor-book listings—you'll place yourself above the licensed crowd.

A final word on purging: It is best that the listing, notwithstanding the "active" versus "pending" language above, be left in order in the book but boldly marked "unavailable," "sold," "pending" or whatever to save a few agents the frustration of trying to find a listing that's here today but gone tomorrow. Alternatively, listing sheets for unavailable properties may be placed in a "dead" category in back of the book for a few weeks to forestall confusion.

*   *   *   *

Thus, we may view our office's floor book and schedule as among the floorperson's greatest resources, resources that remain vital to the livelihood of many agents throughout their careers.

For a young agent, floor time will probably be a mandatory activity, but we hope that the foregoing words will help you see it as a benefit rather than an obligation. There's money to be made and enjoyment to be realized. The caller on the other end of the line isn't calling for fun or to see if you read this chapter. She's in town for the weekend on her company's nickel to scout out homes, and somewhere in that book in front of you (or your MLS book) is her new home's address. Don't hang up until you tell her what it is and make an appointment to show it to her!

Advertising

Soon after opening our modest little brokerage office, we flip-flopped around seeking a corporate slogan, much akin to the big guys'. We tried "We're looking for a few good buyers," then "When better homes are built, Breckenridge will sell them" and later "Better living through brokerage."

Our reward was little save grief and certified mail from the Pentagon, General Motors and DuPont Chemical. We'll not soon tangle with Madison Avenue again.

No siree. We settled on the safe, folksy motto "The transaction went so smooth we bought the company."

* * * *

A free-thinker might conclude, with some merit, that advice about displaying your fashionable new listing on TV during halftime at the Orange Bowl might fall naturally into a chapter about advertising.

While we'd be mortified if we accidentally squelched the creativity of a budding entrepreneur in our midst, the stuff of this chapter will be less of the hype typifying the Pepsi Generation than good old meat-and-potatoes, agent-level advertising in hometown print media. And many ad salespeople, to give credit where it's due, know their media, costs and your market better than we do, so many of our words will be more of an overview than a "how-to"—we'll leave that to local resources.

*   *   *   *

The building block of any ad is an accurate description and representation of the product. And in the real estate business, statistics, although widely varied, confirm that the overwhelming percentage of our advertising is accomplished via the printed word, or at least without the benefit of a photograph or visual representation of that product: Our listing.

It would therefore seem to behoove any agent to get to know the characteristics of a listing by more than a handful of generic terms and adjectives. Architecture is a critical denominator in an informed prospect's mind—"brick veneer" tells her little—that may indicate one or two stories, natural or painted exterior and traditional or modern style (whatever those two mean!). But tell her in an ad that the listing's "Tudor," and she'll know it's red brick, probably two-story with some exposed stucco, a steep roof with dormers and a hobbit door. Or use two words: Tell her it's *Loire Valley*, her clue that it's white brick with a dark or green mansard roof and probably symmetrical, with the entry door centered. In a world where many newspapers base ad rates by the word, *French Quarter* buys a paragraph of information.

The point can be pounded to death, and we needn't offer a dozen examples of each architectural element of the listing from the stemwalls up to the chimney. We will offer two suggestions: First, buy one of a dozen good architectural books, written in lay language and replete with drawings and photographs. (Our contention for years has been that no brokerage office should open its doors without having at least one available!) Find the style and heritage of your listing's design within the book, and carry that information through into your ads and fliers.

The second resource is one of the many home ownership and improvement magazines, and we express a personal view that if a lass or laddie's bound to make a living selling homes, such a magazine subscription is a must. The magazine, arriving each month, showcases not only homes *in toto* but individual features within the homes, stated in commonly accepted nomenclature as it emerges in owners' acceptance. (We once cobrokered a home with a gentleman who was totally amazed by the "orange" appliances in our listing. Had he read anything but *Soldier of Fortune* regularly since entering the business, he'd have know they were "persimmon" and had already been in vogue so long they were on the way out.)

The message: Get to know the homes you're advertising and what our sellers put inside them.

Don't Split Hairs

Now, a simple caution to prevent over-building the building block: The caution is to avoid an *overly* finite description of your listing in the ad. We find that a reasonably accurate description of the home will convey to 98 percent of our targeted prospects what we'd like them to know about the listing. Occasionally the other 2 percent will take exception and point out, correctly, that the home's really "Norman" style, not Tudor. Some parts of our country, particularly the Colonial East Coast, host an ungodly number of minor variations of European influence, but in most ads the better-known description, e.g., "Colonial" or "Tudor," opens the door to an informed conversation. If the callers want to split hairs later over "Antebellum" versus "Reconstruction," you can at least be Civil.

*　*　*　*

With that groundwork laid, we can expand on a few thoughts about agent-initiated residential ads in a number of media. The most frequently used and productive medium is probably the good ol' morning paper.

While you're on hold waiting for the next available ad counselor, look at the home you've described on your clipboard. Travel through the masonry entry columns with the rich patina on the ornamental iron gates, then up the cobblestone drive lined with verdant lawn, statuary and mature trees cloaked in Spanish moss. See the crisp white paint on the shiplap siding, the black slate roof of the arched portico over the Arabesque-glazed window, hear your boots crunch on the Arizona flagstone porch and feel your gloves close on the antique brass latch peened by an artisan a hundred years ago.

Then, when the counselor comes on the line, be ready to tell her of this listing in a dozen words. In a newspaper line ad, where we do most of our day-to-day promotion, that's about how many words you get either to set the hook with prospects or lose them, and that's about how many words you or your broker can afford to run on any consistent basis.

Veteran real estate ad writers, adept at their craft, could probably get the Beach Boys to warm up to an igloo with only a dozen well-chosen words.

*   *   *   *

The text so far should provide an insight into the procedure in most residential offices: Agents are usually expected to write their own ads.

The ads accompany the copy for a new listing to the office sales manager, who verifies the legality and content of the ads and places them into the rotation for placement into the newspaper. (That rotation is an important point of discussion with a manager, and we'll return to it shortly.)

Variation II is placement of the ad on your own if your office permits you to do this. This variant may apply to a small line ad or a larger ad considered by most papers to be in the "display" category, with customized type styles and some sort of border.

In either case, comply with your office's requirements for management approval, but don't stop there: Get a second opinion from another agent in the office, maybe one who has visited the listing—possibly the "backup" agent we'll refer to soon in the "Vacations" chapter. We all see so many homes and write so many ads that they all start blending together after a while. See if your partner has a thought you might have missed.

We promised earlier that we weren't going to compete with other resources and media salespeople and turn this chapter into a "how-to," but we'll sneak in this thought: Look at other listings and advertising currently being run by your office as you are preparing your own ads, and highlight some amenity not appearing in another ad. You're writing the ads to get the phone ringing, and in all probability you may not be the agent to get that call if the ad is running with a number of other ads for other listings with the office's phone number.

The reason for that suggestion is to ensure that if your office currently has two Cape Cod cottages listed and being advertised, your ad will be identifiable. If you have the only cottage with a detached garage, a picket fence or another unique amenity, that feature in the ad will zero the office floorperson in on your listing. (Many offices run an identifier code with text to facilitate location in the floor book—

great, so long as the caller has the paper in hand and is not shooting from the hip with a fuzzy recollection of the ad.)

Play It Straight

An advertising term found in some real estate texts is "puffing," which we assume has its origin in "puffing up" and connotes any statement a tad less than candid but stopping short of a full-blown lie. And we never had a college class adjourn without someone asking where the line between puffing and false advertising was drawn.

We hadn't a real clear response. Given our penchant for using an example to avoid being cornered by answering a question, we offer as an example of puffing the trait of a local coworker, well known for advertising a "Country kitchen" if any feature as remotely rural as simulated woodgrain on a microwave would justify it. Puffing, as a practice, is probably nonprosecutable by a state agency, but it certainly is an annoyance to buyers and other licensees.

False advertising is a horse of another color and needs little attention within these pages. Dissemination of information known to be false or which may be determined to be false by a real estate licensee utilizing tests within the scope of his or her training against situations usual to our practice, awakens the gargoyle of false advertising, which will eventually turn and bite both you and your broker.

Some real estate people would have the public believe that there are more view lots in America during the winter months than in the summer. Don't be the agent who forgets that leaves burst from the branches of trees each spring, and the only view thereafter will be the tree. Call it puffing or a falsehood, but don't call it a view lot!

*   *   *   *

Somewhere between patent puffing and pure prevarication rests the tickler many of us put into an ad now and again, probably for fun and maybe just to see if anybody is *really* reading the ads we pay so dearly for.

We once pitched a listing with a microwave fireplace and found that more respondents were irritated than heartwarmed to learn that such a device would enable a couple to spend an entire evening by the fire in less than 40 minutes.

We were glad then that we didn't throw in our smoke alarm with a five-minute snooze button.

Federal Conformance

We'll take a brief look at a totally different avenue to false advertising, an avenue taken by almost all of us occasionally, inadvertently and with no malice intended. Examples and scenarios can run out to perpetuity and even then are subject to some interpretation, so we won't belabor the words, but we will throw one key word out, a word to watch like a hawk when you're writing an ad.

The word is *interest*.

Bear in mind all that you learned in real estate school about the weird and wonderful things that can impact interest on a loan during an assumption or when nonrecurring costs are amortized into any amount paid at close of escrow that does not reduce the principal.

Be guided by the 1974 Real Estate Settlement and Procedures Act (RESPA) and the Truth-in-Lending Act of Federal Regulation Z/226.1 (our old friend "Reg. Z," and the "Z" ain't for Zorro). American might be the world's only language wherein the verb "to Z" may be integrated into an industry.

An alternate resource concerning TIL: input from your manager or a lending institution officer. Best of all: Avoid any references to interest when offering financing information in your ads. Unless the content is clear-cut and pure as the driven snow, which few situations are, a discussion can wait until you can offer a prospect an accurate portrayal of interest benefits after she's responded to your ad.

*   *   *   *

A minor point, but one that could rapidly upgrade to major during your career: In the records chapter we emphasized the need to commit copies of *all* advertising or motivational information to your listing's file, and we reinforce the suggestion (the *mandate* in some states) in this advertising chapter.

You may write an accurate ad on a rather complex home, then later be taken to task by a responder who misunderstood the content of that ad (or flier, within the context of this chapter). It's nice to have a copy of the ad handy within your own office, saving the need to tear the local paper's morgue asunder to get yourself off the hook.

And, to repeat the advice offered earlier, save *all* advertising—not just that which results in a conveyance.

Advertisement Frequency

A page or two ago we promised to serve up a topic to include in a pre-association interview with a potential new manager. The topic was the rotation of ads, which now equates to *frequency* of office-placed newspaper advertising. And hand-in-hand with frequency of ads comes *payment* for the ads. In a close third place is a discussion of any other office-supported advertising available for your listings.

As is our usual intent when suggesting questions to ask interviewing brokers, we'll not offer solutions but be content to ignite a few fuses that should touch off a revealing discussion with each of them.

And, within the stated confines of the chapter, we're staying within newspaper (line) ads—the denominator of most of our early-career efforts. If your town and the office you're interviewing with fits the greater American pattern, the office probably runs an ad several days a week containing a small number of listings, then a blockbuster in the Saturday or Sunday real estate supplement, with an expanded number of listings featured.

And thus are suggested the first fuses: "How often will my listing be advertised?" "Will it be given priority in the first weekend supplement following listing?"

The response to the latter question is usually "yes." The first question, however, is a little trickier. The prudent sales manager (sometimes mutually exclusive terms) would hold to a strict, mindless rotation, with all office listings placed in order and no reinsertions until all listings have been advertised.

However, in some offices larger producers are rewarded with accelerated rotation of their listings' ads. Or another office may target a geographical area or a price range in any one group of ads—your listing could potentially fall outside of these bounds. You'll no doubt be reminded of this omission by the sellers, a species known to meet the kid with the papers at dawn's early light every morning until their home sells.

No answers here, just questions to be raised, with responses forming just one indicator for comparing candidate offices. (And sales managers take note: Don't be offended. We were one, for Coldwell Banker, for a year and prudently listened to every screwball reason and plea under the sun to run an agent's listing out of sequence.)

Office-Supported Advertising

The natural follow-up to the preceding questions is: "Who pays?" We know of offices, and you'll ferret out a few more, that offer splits that inordinately favor the agent. But investigate wisely—in many cases those offices do not fully support the individual agent's advertising needs.

The most desirable situation from the agent's point of view is office-paid advertising in an equitable rotation with other agents and as devoid as possible of favoritism. Should an agent wish to augment office-supported advertising on any one listing, he or she may request additional insertions to be billed to the office at the office's contract rate (usually a lower per-word or per-line price than available to the agent as an individual). Such additional advertising will appear as a charge to the agent on a monthly office statement—convenient to the agent, the office's bookkeeper and Uncle Sam.

Not quite so nifty but a real motivator for the less-than-industrious agent, is agent-paid advertising, placed in the office's regular ad groupings, billed at contract rate to the office by the paper and passed through to the agent on a monthly basis. Upon conveyance of the listing, funds spent by the agent for advertising the listing are directed back to the agent by some prearranged formula, ranging from matching funds upward to full recompensation.

*   *   *   *

A final category, not to enumerate the myriad variations possible from full-ride to this one, the low rung on the ladder: The office doesn't advertise. Or it allows agents to group ads under the office logo, and maybe it has a contract and administers charges out among the agents, but it pays no costs. There are a few offices who don't participate in advertising—if an agent's split is high, office advertising may not be available.

In defense of some of these offices, we should reveal that their clientele and/or market area, or their agent roster, may not indicate a need for newspaper line advertising. In those cases, the many are relieved of the burden of subsidizing the few who rely on line ads.

*   *   *   *

A hearty discussion of advertising cooperation will probably result in clarification of some of the following topics and might even result in a few coming to light that we haven't mentioned. Feel free to put questions about some of the thoughts that follow to any prospective manager.

In some areas the supermarket-distributed, tabloid-style fliers, many with expanded descriptive text, geographical organization and full-color artwork, have become tremendously effective. In fact, in these areas the failure of an agent to utilize an established tabloid is tantamount to exercising less than a fully effective standard of practice in marketing. And this could be a good time to throw out one of our longstanding opinions: If a seller thinks that you'd be derelict in not using tabloid (or any other form of) advertising, and you and your manager fail to see a material benefit other than inflating the seller's ego, you may remind the seller that paying for advertising is a game two can play—he can compensate you for running superfluous ads.

A word to the wise: Should a seller utter the ugly words "deficient standard of practice," "lack of diligence" or recognizable variations of same, call the boss and convene a meeting with your principals and get everybody's expectations straight.

Judge for yourself the advantage of tabloid advertising in your own market area, using their level of success in stimulating inquiries against yours. They're not cheap, but they may be effective. And check to see if there is broker participation in your office.

Seller Participation

We broached the subject of seller participation in your advertising, and that concept calls for a huge caveat: Do allow the sellers to help you pay for advertising over and above what you and your office are willing and able to provide, but *DON'T* allow a seller to write, design or place any advertising or other form of motivational material targeted to the general public without your prior approval. (Or your broker's!)

Veterans in the business convene periodically to swap horror stories, and a recurrent favorite is always a recollection of inaccurate or illegal motivational language about a listing placed by a well-meaning and possibly well-heeled seller in a company newspaper, on the flanks of an elephant at a convention or blinking along the fuselage of a blimp idling low over the Santa Monica Freeway at rush hour.

The sellers only want to help, but their over-zealousness is not tempered by a license, and you're responsible for their actions (somewhat). So tell them that the help is appreciated, but you'd like a peek at their brainstorm first.

*   *   *   *

Thus far, aside from vital references to blimps and pachyderms, we've been mostly concerned with the printed word—newspapers and tabloids. These outlets, together with yard signs, which we don't contemplate as the stuff of this chapter, form the nucleus of our efforts to get word of availability out to the world.

Two derivatives of yard signs *are* of marginal interest for inclusion here: One is a sign configured to hold fliers about the home right on the sign so a potential drive-by prospect can take a brochure about the listing for future consideration. We've no opinion inasmuch as we've never used them nor talked with anyone who has; but somewhere they're probably being used to an agent's benefit.

But the really slick idea, ditto on having encountered an agent who's used them, is the yard sign with the little radio transmitter putting out about 1 watt of power and sporting a written notice advising drive-bys to tune to some frequency on the AM band for information about the home. They've been advertised in trade publications for years, so somewhere in this land they must be here to stay!

Advertise Yourself!

We take a new tack now in the brief pages remaining in this chapter. Until now our text has been of listings—conveyance of information about a specific product: A known home. And it's been only a brief overview, not in competition with the myriad of other advertising resources.

The new course steers toward what most call "institutional" advertising—advertising and promoting good will favoring the merchant, not his or her wares. In a nutshell, we're talking "name recognition."

As a newer agent, you might not be tapped for the responsibility of furthering your office's image around town, but for a relative pittance you may do wonders for your own personal "institution." In our town, and most probably yours, service clubs, youth groups, professional or business associations and sporting event organizers all line up three deep to sell business-card-size advertising in programs. Most real estate agents agree that these are one of the more valuable advertising resources available.

A few small, semipermanent signs are also nice, and the cost can be spread among a few agents if you all want to throw in together. (A reminder about this and other strategies for getting your name out: Reread the "names" chapters if necessary, but do display your name(s) properly in conjunction with your office's.)

You may not be ready for a small space on the scoreboard at Wrigley Field, but if you live and work in a quiet little town with a hometown stadium, ice rink or golf course, display rates are usually reasonable.

For about a dollar a day in our town, an agent or group can advertise on a bus bench, and for very little more they can get their name driven all over town on the bus itself. (Legally. We'll not advocate graffiti.) And if you don't like mass transit, an option is the magnetic car sign we discuss in the automobile chapter coming up next.

*   *   *   *

Our final offering in a chapter of topics that could go on forever, begins with a paean that would appear to be lifted from the Great Words of Andy Rooney. We've not seen this theme in his columns, but it sounds so like him that we'll apologize in advance just in case he beat us to it.

The simple thought is that if we want a T-shirt advertising Vaurnet sunglasses or Nike shoes, we go out and pay twelve bucks for it. A certain ski hill in Colorado once charged us nine dollars for a baseball cap with our own surname on it. Yet if we want others to wear a T-shirt with "Breckenridge Realty," or some variant of that name printed on it, *we* pay twelve dollars to have it made, and good luck in selling it to your client.

To close this chapter on advertising and promotion on our usual serious note, we'll confirm what many have found to be true: The cost of a few imprinted shirts or hats with the name of the office river-rafting team or golf foursome will be returned to you many times over. Generously offer them. And have a little fun with the imprinted gadgets you can order in advertising specialty stores—most of them are inexpensive.

A schoolmate of ours ran for the state senate, and while we're hard pressed to be in the same room with him if an alternative exists, the refrigerator magnets he campaigned with have made him a household word.

Name recognition ploys belong only questionably in a chapter on advertising, so we've spread them equally over the "names" and the "business development" chapters. But they're an integral part of our business and if orchestrated with minor dosages of subtlety and taste and a fair amount of innovation, and then coupled with intelligent product advertising, they can keep your career rolling along.

*   *   *   *

Away, then—don dusters and goggles. This chapter showed an ugly sign of turning into work for a few paragraphs. We're off to cruise our market area in the motorcar for a little relaxation.

8

The Automobile

As a Prelude to this treatise on a real estate agent's auto, this note of Caprice: Whether you're on the way to Escort a Celebrity or a Diplomat, a Legend or only a lone Ranger, whether she's a New Yorker clad in Sable or has a Continental flair, wear your office Blazer with pride and affect a Regal air; be as observant as an Eagle, as swift as a Jaguar, as Valiant as a Samurai and stay as knowledgeable of Suburban property as that in downtown Malibu.

Datsun 'nuff of this Sonata—work at a brisk Tempo, stay in high Spirit and you won't stand the Silver Ghost of a chance of not being Accord-ed success and Acclaim in your new endeavor!

* * * *

If a reader bought this book because she just earned a real estate license and is now seeking advice on what manner of new wheels to buy, we counsel her to return the book to her bookseller before the pages get dog-eared and find a more appropriate work in the stacks of the occult, the mystic and the unknown. The sole vehicular truism we can share with you is that parked in every real estate marketplace across the land there is what once was a fine auto, now slightly dated by fender skirts, a pointy hood ornament or a two-piece windshield. To keep the whole chapter in perspective, we'll reveal that this relic is probably the workhorse of one of the town's more prolific real estate professionals. It isn't that she chooses to drive it; she's just too busy selling houses to shop for another car.

*   *   *   *

We won't belabor the obvious fact that you should have a car that's safe and comfortable. Nor will we push a big sedan or a compact, an import or made-in-Motown; nor will we rule out a pickup or a two-seat sports car—there have been too many successful agents delivered to the scene of the sale in all conceivable conveyances. (We have a friend who seems able to sell more property riding a Harley-Davidson than he can in his car.) We will tell you that as you advance in your career, you'll note that property "listers" and "sellers" have differing preferences in transportation. Those who primarily list homes have less need for commodious carriages than the "sellers," who spend a good part of their day with guests on board.

A curious motivation that a friend found for selecting a car was a perceived need to be able to haul some of her fellow agents in style on Wednesday morning office tours of newly listed properties. This necessity doesn't loom large in too many agents' minds, and in fact many vow after their first office-caravan tour that they will never again take their own cars on these journeys unless they first gird them with junk tires à la New York Harbor tugboats. The convoy delivering a large office's sales crew to a cul-de-sac listing rivals the excitement of a demolition derby at the county fair.

Seating and Styling

A few random thoughts about choice of a real estate agent's car: The obvious, all-kidding-aside fact is that once in a while even Mr. or Ms. 100 percent Listing Agent gets cornered into having to take more than one person somewhere, even if it's just to the escrow company, and we'd hate to blow a sale because the only thing in the motor pool was a two-seat convertible. If you can conduct 99 percent of your business in the MG, good for you, but have an ace in the hole ready for the occasional unexpected sales opportunity when you're faced with squiring more than one client across town.

Some of the real dream wheels have a propensity for "backing off" a prospect. We're no different from anyone in any other sales business in that we view our car as an extension of our personality and productivity. Nevertheless, we must be somewhat mindful of the public's perception of us as members of an industry.

There's a loosely defined upper limit of how good a first impression we have to make with our typical customers. Homesellers of modest means might view any of us arriving at a listing appointment in an Aston-Martin with more a feeling of intimidation than a perception of success. We owned a fire-engine red German roadster for nine years and eventually learned that the family wagon was almost consistently the better car for day-to-day real estate, not for the size advantage but to allay our clients' resistance to our sybaritic lifestyle.

So drive what you will, drive what you already own or buy whatever turns you on if you need a new car. But never lose sight of the fact that the most important factor in success isn't the car itself but the developing professional at the helm.

*   *   *   *

We'll be brief on another point: A clean car is a happy car. Inside and out. We have some friends in and out of real estate with classy wheels, but when they pick us up for lunch, we feel like we are visiting the inside of a goat's stomach, clearing a pathway to the seat through jogging clothes, dog hair, newspapers, fast-food styro boxes with half-consumed mystery meat and other general debris. "We are what we drive" is a disgruntling thought by comparison to the more appropriate measures of a professional, but if the thought's valid, an advance team with a litter bag and Dustbuster should be dispatched to the nether regions of the limousine every now and then.

Insurance

Thus far we've approached the car as a marketing tool, the aforementioned revelation of an agent's personality and success to an inquiring public. We'll drift back to that soon, but now an important point about a licensee's car, be it clean or dirty, large, small, new or ancient: Insure the car with a reputable insurance carrier, and keep the insurance in force at all costs when you are using your car in the furtherance of your business endeavors.

In all probability if you own a car, you are already carrying insurance, but as you step over the threshold from pleasure driving to business use, your insurance agent should be informed of the amended use of the vehicle. Time after time when talking this over with first-year agents, we have found that they are reluctant to bring the new business use to their agent's attention for fear of being faced with a premium increase.

We'll not put words into the mouths of our barrister and insurance adjustor friends, but we'll offer a clue as to what they might say: The insurer's exposure is elevated when the passengers in your car become contractual occupants, and insurers do not react kindly to surprises about their policyholders' business endeavors. It doesn't take a major accident with severe bodily injury for you to wind up facing a claim; check with your agent, and you'll probably find that your passengers are covered by your insurance when they are entering, occupying or alighting from your car. Thus, a simple twisted ankle suffered by a prospect on an icy driveway could put you into a coverage situation.

The message is to play it straight with your agent prior to trundling your first prospect off to her dream home. Tell the agent about your business connection, and if you own a second car, decide whether you'll be using both cars with clients. (For most of us, that's almost inevitable.) The up-side is the peace of mind of knowing you're covered, that the increase in premium is negligible and the best news: Your agent might send you a referral, and one commission buys a lot of car insurance!

Footnote to managers, if you're peeking into this book: It's not a bad idea to spot-check your agents' insurance coverages once in a while. If an unfortunate situation turned consummately ugly, a member of the public injured in your agent's vehicle might look to your firm for redress if your agent's insurance had lapsed or coverage was declined for any reason.

Cars Have Trunks—Let's Use Them!

We credit ex-Raider football-coach-turned-sportscaster John Madden with helping put the next words into focus: The prose he dumped into our lap one afternoon while the Bears were getting theirs told the difference between the sophisticated quarterback-technicians and the down-and-dirty interior linemen. Our analogy equates quarterbacks with real estate agents in training videotapes and TV ads, arriving in a spiffy-clean car with all four hubcaps intact and stepping out of that car in impeccable clothes (he in a sport coat and tie and she in a bow-blouse, office blazer and catchy-but-businesslike coif). They both are smiling and happy and have leather cases full of appropriate real estate forms. We like all that in an agent, but let's see what the All-Breckenridge team—which includes linemen—throws in the trunks of their cars.

In reality, nylon bags like the ones airlines used to give away are usually big enough to hold some of the tools of the trade seldom seen in real estate TV commercials. What we're trying to achieve is a degree of self-sufficiency when we're out in the field—to create a rolling office, with some creature comforts to deal with everyday challenges. Let's fill a bag with some tools and tricks to make the interior line of real-life real estate go smoother.

*   *   *   *

Recall the times when you'd have given your kingdom for a pair of pliers to turn just one nut; let that thought develop. The pliers, maybe a crescent wrench, a safe knife, a Phillips and a flat screwdriver and a light hammer might help you cure some small problem not worth calling a repairman for and give you something to do during a slow open house. A pigtail circuit tester can determine whether a plug is working or which plug is wired to a light switch. Buyers are convinced that all houses are out of plumb—so throw in an eight-inch level—maybe the buyer's right and the door jamb needs attention.

We suggest two kinds of measuring tapes—one, a 24-foot spring-return type, long enough to measure the largest interior areas. The thin version is a little lighter and easier to control; and a 1-inch wide tape will last longer. You might just as well form the habit of taking it with you on your belt or in your purse on serious showing appointments or inevitably be faced with a trip back to the car when the client wants to know whether a breakfront will fit on a particular wall.

A slight digression: Not to undermine your real estate instructor's good work, but if you've passed the state test, you are now permitted to forget that there are 43,560 square feet in an acre and commit to memory that a queen-size bed is 60 inches by 80 inches and a standard door is 6 feet, 8 inches high. Familiarity with the measurements of common appliances and furniture (most of which are standardized) will make your day-to-day life easier than your instant recall of the number of rods in a chain. (Or is it chains in a rod?)

And now back to tapes, type II: A crank-rewind, 50-foot or 100-foot tape is good for exterior measurements of the longer distances that frequently interest potential buyers or for measuring the home or yard for value determination. While 50 feet is usually enough, the 100-footer isn't that much more in money or weight. The two scales available are "conventional," in feet and inches, and "engineer's," in feet and tenths of feet. The engineering scale is easier for many of us once we're used to it. Calculating the area of a room that measures 6'9'' by 12'6'' is a two-step process made much easier by a tape that reads the distance as 6.75' by 12.50'. The choice of scale is yours, but bite the bullet early, buy the tape and keep it in your real estate bag. You'll use it.

And pack a third tape, not the measuring kind: Disposable surveyor's or engineer's tape (resembling a nylon ribbon) in a bright Day-Glo color such as orange or lime-green. It's sold in rolls an inch wide and long enough that two rolls will probably last through a real estate career; it tears easily without scissors. We keep a couple of rolls handy to close off verboten areas of a home or yard during open houses, to mark unsafe areas (ice and snow or construction) and to call attention to distant parts of a yard, such as a property corner stake.

Worth a Thousand Words

No real estate agent worth their salt would go out of the office without a camera, but here's an alternative to taking the expensive, full-size (and weight) family Canon, Olympus, Minolta, whatever, everywhere you go, night and day: Go out today and buy a $20 camera and throw it in your traveling bag. Many veterans have found that such photos, while not the finest, do a credible job for real estate purposes. The cameras offer the luxury of being cheap enough to be lost, dropped or totally demolished, and a busy agent will probably go through one a year.

We once had prospects who commiserated that they came to town to look for homes without bringing their own camera, so we gave them ours, a beat-up Instamatic already on its last legs. (We're passing up the temptation to tell you that we shutter to think how old that thing was or how many Brownie points we made with it...) We never saw the camera again, but we sold them a mega-home and consider the transaction on balance to be just dandy.

Final note on cameras: We frequently see agents scrambling to get pictures of homes processed so the buyer can take them home on the plane to show a spouse. Unless your buyer lives in a town without a photo shop, just give them the exposed roll, finished or not, and let them have it developed at leisure. (If they're flying, put it in luggage, not carry-on.)

*   *   *   *

Our bag is slowly filling, but while the models in the real estate commercial smile at the TV audience, let's see what else the real-life agent with rolled-up sleeves can put to good use in a typical day.

Some say maps might go in the leather case on the front seat and not in the working bag, but somewhere in your car carry area maps— not just one, but extras that you can mark up with schools, work-places, home locations, freeway access and anything else the buyers want to see. A high-light marker is great for this—throw one in the bag. Put a couple of good quality markers in too, along with a pack of five-by-eight-inch cards to make feature or warning signs or signs indicating property not included in the sale for showings and open houses. Throw in some Scotch tape to fasten them up and to attach notes and cards to doors and windshields on a windy day. Isn't it great to be ready for anything when we go to work!

We formed a habit years ago of keeping some self-addressed, stamped envelopes at the ready, not necessarily in our "brain bag," as we call our worn-out airline/tool bag, but in the front of both cars, at the office and around the house. It's awfully easy for a friend to honor your request to send you some information she has access to if you put a stamped envelope right in her hand. The cost is minor in comparison to the mutual convenience.

We usually keep a flashlight bagged up for peering around dark areas, basements, crawl spaces and attics. And, somewhere it's written that places that are dark are usually dirty or dusty, suggesting a need for a few towels or rags for you or your prospects' dirty hands.

The last suggestion for your bag is a phone book, included for several reasons: First, books in phone booths are frequently ripped up or missing altogether. Remember, we're trying to create a mini-office in your car from which you can do business until you can return to the mother ship. A better reason to carry a phone book is that the telephone companies nationwide are increasing the scope of their directories to include a wealth of information about local areas: Schools, government, public transportation, parks and senior facilities—a veritable fountain of knowledge.

That's a small sampling of what we have in our bag—an airport metal detector's nightmare were the bag to take flight. We'll leave it to you what to put in yours, but we hope you'll benefit from the suggestions as you slip into a phone booth and metamorphose from an impeccably-dressed super-salesperson into a player at the scrimmage line, where we spend most of our time (and find most of our reward!).

Stick with Signs

No child in today's America should have to grow up in a town where the local real estate people don't use magnetic office signs on their cars. How else would these youngsters, so eager to learn of their world, be able to determine just how many objects on earth are made of ferrous metal?

Cars, of course, are steel, like your car and mine—and fully capable of hosting a magnetic sign. Dumpsters are steel, as are some phone booths, lockers in schools and clubs and most truck bodies. Boxcars are steel so we could, theoretically, send a Coldwell Banker sign from Reno to some classmates in Atlanta as a hands-across-the-nation signal of good will. We've seen a marriage of Century 21 and Ma Bell and heard of another between Better Homes and Gardens and the Reno Police Department—Pac Tel and R.P.D. all use steel cars, too.

We'll make the assumption that the larger justification for a magnetic sign on a car is for advertising and let most of the thoughts that such an assumption connotes reside within the previous advertising chapter. BUT:

Advertising value notwithstanding, a major advantage of signage on your car as you go about your business is to identify car and driver as real estate-related. We discovered the value of this in the mid-1960s when we had a little property management company and our duties frequently dispatched us in the early morning hours to a pitch-black parking lot to cure some problem or another within a building. When the police see a parked pickup, a ladder against the wall and a flashlight gyrating around the roof at three in the morning, they are seldom inclined to think it's the Fuller Brush Man. We bought a set of signs to identify ourself and went from negotiation with the full SWAT team to merely one or two reasonable men and women of Reno's Finest.

The typical residential brokerage agent's hours are seldom as weird as a commercial property manager's, but in showing homes we do a lot of stop, slow, back up, turn around in a neighbor's driveway, wait, talk and then do it all over again as we show a prospect a home or neighborhood. A homeowner looking out of a window might think us eccentric, and a mag sign on the car may not prove her assumption wrong; but it tells her that at least we are licensed by our state to be eccentric, which might put her mind at ease.

* * * *

Another thought about signs is that they are not painted onto the car but only temporarily attached and removable, a fact forgotten by many magnetic sign users. There's a time to boldly display your office affiliation and another time to hide your light under a bushel. We fear that our sons probably did unspeakable things with our Suburban in their early driving years, and while we didn't endorse or approve, the last thing we needed was to identify this 6,000-pound station wagon streaking through the night as even remotely related to Breckenridge Realty.

Many of us in the business regard certain occasions where automobiles congregate to be outside the bounds of tasteful advertising: Two good examples are church parking lots and funeral processions. A little pitch for the business is fine at the Little League park, but other events transcend the bounds of commerce, and the signs are best left home on the garage door or metal cabinet.

No Bubble-Top Limos

We learned this next fact from prospects-turned-friends and not from only one isolated client but a number of them who have expressed variations of this opinion: Prospects frequently feel uncomfortable enough when home shopping in an unfamiliar town and meeting a series of homeowners whose homes they tour, without having to ride around in a marked car like a trophy tuna slung from the yardarm for all to see as the boat glides into harbor. Several clients have told us over the years that they would have declined to accompany us in their search for a home if our car had been identified as an agent's car.

Ask around in your market area—you might find that veterans have received similar feedback from buyers. A rule of thumb might be that signs are great in normal running around or when keeping a listing appointment but could cause a prospect some anxiety and perhaps should be left at home or in the trunk when working with buyers.

A final word on car signs: Think about personal security, if you please. Some offices have policies about this topic, the topic being an agent's name and *home phone number* displayed in conjunction with the office name and logo. Many of us are a little jumpy about being *too* available to the public, and it's probably going to take more than a phone number on a car sign to get a bona fide prospect to call. The majority of the calls you might get, veterans have learned, are those you don't need.

He Just Doesn't Relish Mustard

Thus our automotive segment approaches an off-ramp, and we're going to take it. It's been a good trip. We learned that a car isn't all that important, but we do deserve a nice one, for ourselves first, then for our clients. It should be clean and insured and stocked with a few tools to get us through the day. And our signs are great fun for the adolescents and of possible benefit to our business recognition. But a truly skilled agent can still sell like crazy using the hood of an Edsel as a desktop.

Before setting the brakes, we'll witness the plight of fellow broker and close friend George Hatjakes, who bought an impeccable midnight-blue Rolls-Royce Silver Shadow recently. The decade-old beauty was used as a limousine by Harrah's Tahoe, and the Connolly-leather seats had no doubt molded to the backsides of many of the most prominent superstars of the 1970s and early 1980s. The car is a true classic, and our friend indeed caught the brass ring of his real estate career. The Rolls brings him great pleasure, for he is a stout man, and the car is commodious, a resurrection of a bygone era of motoring—certainly the culmination of his real estate endeavors.

But after a month, George is already thinking of selling it. His real estate stature might have been elevated through ownership of the car—that jury's still out. But this verdict's in: Don't be the next person to stop alongside him and ask for a jar of Grey Poupon. He's heard that before, several times now, and his response is showing signs of turning downright mean.

9

Vacations

Veteran agents endorse a foolproof but expensive technique to move a flurry of inactivity off dead center: They plop themselves across a desk from their travel agent and buy a couple of Super-Saver airline tickets to whisk them off to Hawaii, where a beachfront condominium will await them.

The term "non-refundable" figures heavily into this career jumpstart—the cost of the tickets and the condo deposit, once paid, must disappear into the mist like the view of Haleakala from the condo at dawn's first light.

*   *   *   *

Polynesian legend has it that the planned-vacation syndrome has never failed the idle real estate agent. The chime an agent hears as the vacation begins usually isn't the captain turning off the seat belt sign but a fellow salesperson phoning with a near-asking-price offer on a listing that hasn't been shown for many weeks. *Mahalo,* buyer, but *aloha* travel deposits.

*   *   *   *

Most readers would agree that it's ridiculous to call off a trip just to present an offer and secure an acceptance from the sellers. After all, our procedures are fairly standard and predictable, and there are other salespeople in the office who'd be happy to handle it for you. We'll meet with your sellers, you call the cab and scurry to the airport and we'll all settle up upon your suntanned, pudgy reincarnation on the Mainland.

We all do these trade-offs frequently, and with practice and a little forethought, we can banish the white knuckles from real estate and relegate them back to the airliner where they belong. In this chapter the text suggests a bit of systemic cross-training of the other agents in your office about your listings *prior* to the time your bags are packed and the cab's on the way. We aren't making reference to the "buddy system," a common and frequently successful alliance of two (or more) agents who act as a team and frequently share earned income. While the buddy system is an approach to vacation coverage, many agents look more for short-term assistance than a year-round partnership.

A second observation: This chapter is written as if you were the departee—as you read, remember, you may be the one left behind in the "backup agent" role. The text is applicable in either situation.

A "Backup" Agent

Let's back up several months prior to planning this little *hukilau* with the travel agent and glance around your sales office. You'll note that your fellow salespeople are not all created equal—there are those who list and those who sell, some who like farms and ranches, others who do urban properties. We know condo specialists, duplex or apartment whizzes, fixer-upper experts and a few with a full range of experience from cottages to castles. Personalities also abound: Our coworkers may be sports nuts or understand the stock market or the symphony or golf or live in your listing's neighborhood or would love to see the Wurlitzer in your client's game room. In short, you work with an aggregation of humans, all as different as night and day.

One of the many hats a canny salesperson wears is the cap of a matchmaker—a *yentl*, if our recollection of "Fiddler on the Roof" serves us correctly. We match our clients with the persona of another agent in our office. The match might work because the agent is the resident expert on the client's Victorian home, or it might have less to do with the listed property than the fact that the agent's son plays basketball with the seller's boy—a strictly personal thread. In either case, we create a bond between a backup agent and our clients.

*   *   *   *

We like to take the chosen agent to the listing and introduce her to the owners. Her input about marketing the home can't hurt a bit, and it puts another set of eyes, ears and recollections about the listing into our office in case we're out and a call comes about the property. We've had sellers confide to us that they were reassured in knowing that the entire marketing plan for their home didn't revolve around one agent waiting by his phone. And if our backup partner calls to make a showing appointment, she has the benefit of an established personal relationship with the owners.

Thus, when the selling agent phoned simultaneously with the airport taxi arrival in our driveway, we were comfortable in telling that agent to call our backup compadre. She was forewarned that our mind was already at 30,000 feet, and our sellers appreciated being left in capable, informed hands. The selling agent and the buyer were accorded the businesslike treatment they deserve from our office.

Everyone came out winners in this transaction—the sellers felt good about our service, and in a few paragraphs we'll reveal that our backup agent didn't exactly do this out of the goodness of her heart. But as the great silver bird swung us onto the active runway and the captain requested clearance west to Kahului, her compensation seemed a small price to pay. This vacation was possible because we planned ahead.

Assemble a Team

Now we'll tie up a few loose ends: The initial thought is that you probably will have more than one listing in force each time you want to slip out of town, and the likelihood is good that they will vary significantly in terms of physical character, neighborhood and the personality of the owners. It's therefore possible and probably desirable that more than one agent in your office will be affected by your departure and should be briefed about the status of each listing. (Most agents can handle one and maybe two extra listings for a week or so, but dumping your whole inventory on one set of shoulders could be a burden.)

A part of what makes the backup system work is informing all the staffers in the office that a) you're gone, and b) who's handling each of your listings. You should certainly take great pains to make the division of responsibility clear to your sales manager and office secretary, and the floor book should be marked for the benefit of any agent taking an ad or sign call on your listing. Many larger offices have devised fairly comprehensive systems and bulletins for charting the comings and goings of agents.

*   *   *   *

A minor note: Smaller, and even one-person brokerage offices devise similar plans to cover activity while someone is absent. Small offices form a partners-in-arms allegiance in most parts of the country and compete with each other hammer-and-tong while all the principals are in town. But when one goes on vacation and call-forwards his or her messages to a competitor, the others holster their carbines and help out their absent pal. These adversaries usually do an excellent job of covering the empty office until that broker's return. Then the gloves come off and they all go at it again. We owners of mini-offices perpetually amaze and amuse brokers of larger firms with our small-office antics and camaraderie.

Payment

The toughest element of vacation coverage has to be the equitable compensation of the backup agent. We'd love to assemble an equation, factoring in the definable hours expended by the backup agent, the selling commission, the hours and advertising spent by the vacationing agent, whether the backup opened the escrow and the endless number of potential paths the transaction took before a commission was generated. Or we could consider all of the above ultimately resulting in no escrow or commission but with just as much time and commitment. Other conceivable activities by the backup agent can include time spent counseling the seller during the listing agent's absence or attending to listed, vacant property.

There are no hard and fast rules, only realities. The first reality is that every agent in your town must leave that town once in a while or eventually risk being coaxed down from the ceiling of her office. Reality II is that when he or she does leave, she leaves listings behind, and our fiduciary obligation with the sellers demands that somebody affords them the same high degree of diligence; or restated: Life Goes On. Reality III is that some other licensee must obviously pinch-hit for them in their absence, and that pinch-hitter deserves to be paid.

Some say it's a reciprocal thing—you cover me and I'll cover you. But experience indicates that an imbalance usually results, followed by a few hard feelings. Money is nice, and some offices have a policy setting forth a prearranged and fixed percentage of the commission involved. There's probably an occasional inequity created therein, but it's a definite step toward order.

Compensation dictated by each case might be best, predetermined to an extent, with some attempt to equate time-spent to per-hour worth for an agent's assistance where no commission resulted, and tempered by the transaction's complexity and sale price of the property when the assistance led to a conveyance.

*   *   *   *

A caveat to observe is the statute of most states that prohibits a licensee from accepting compensation from any entity other than their own employing broker. We can run afoul of this no-no in a trice if we make any substantial compensation directly to a fellow agent for their help. (Or if we accept substantial sums *from* them.) We usually take the Breckenridge Bailout Team to a good lunch upon returning from one of our flights of fancy, whether or not they did anything to deserve a Big Mac. And if one of these stalwarts actually *did* do something noteworthy, a gift certificate from Macy's can be a nice thank-you. The statutes don't try to regulate courtesy and friendship.

But if serious work occurred and some real money should change hands, the broker should handle the ensuing commission division. A deduction from the vacationer's share directed to the stay-at-home who held the transaction together, all recorded in the broker's account books, will keep both agents in line with the state requirement. And an IRS 1099 from the broker to each party at year's end will reflect the correct incomes and enable each to file their tax return accurately. We want to compensate our fellow agents generously for their help, but we'd just as soon not pay their income tax too!

The vacation coverage and compensation subject is broad, vital and probably oversimplified here, but it is a topic worth discussing with your manager with an eye toward future vacations. Seek your manager's counsel prior to selecting a backup and taking off on vacation, or before taking over and overseeing another agent's business. It's nice to end a vacation on a high note, with your coworkers, and a check waiting for you on your desk!

10

Custodial Listings

Scarcely a real estate agent exists across this favored land who hasn't learned to hit a neighborhood in top hat and tails, à la Professor Harold Hill arriving in River City, to transfer a ragtag collection of neighbor kids into a band of 76 Toros, mowing in unison across the lawn of a brand new listing.

*   *   *   *

One of the larger single motivators for locating a buyer for a home *tout suite* remains the sight of the sellers motoring off in a cloud of dust, leaving you with the care, custody and control of their home until it sells. Vacant homes (or "unoccupied" homes—a more desirable euphemism if an insurance underwriter might be eavesdropping) are a good source of business, and many agents court relocated homeowners or their employers' relocation agencies as a specialty form of clientele.

Whether an agent seeks out vacated homes as listings or happens to list one only infrequently, they are a fact of life that we all encounter occasionally. To put the chapter in perspective, envision a home with the furniture and personal property removed *in toto*—that's how we usually list them. Only infrequently do homeowners leave any appreciable property behind (an exception may be those who have a vacation home to relocate to while your listing's for sale). The next few pages address a cold, lonely listing, with the warmth of the former family long gone down the Interstate. We're going to sell it, but the primary thrust of this chapter is to protect the seller's physical asset.

*   *   *   *

There are several schools of thought about caring for a seller's home while we try to market it, and one of them is that by accepting responsibility, the agent undertakes too large a job with tremendous implications in order to (hopefully) earn a commission. That point's well taken and, in fact, forms the policy of several offices we've known—the broker, ultimately liable for acts and omissions of his or her agents, just doesn't want the responsibility of a vacant home.

And we agree that if the home's too much for one nonresident to care for *in absentia* or has some weird feature that elevates the difficulty, it's probably best to leave the custody to others and concentrate on the marketing function. If the owners want a free salesperson/housesitter, let someone else list it. There are worse occurrences than losing a listing once in a while.

But another observation: We've never seen a rule that a listing agent can't wear two hats—one of a salesperson, the second of a custodial agent. A salesperson usually receives a commission upon conveyance, a custodian some other form of agreed-upon fee, which could be per week or per month, for predetermined services.

A Business Builder

The choices are yours (and your broker's) as you dive headlong into your first custodial listing. Many agents use the service rendered and their expertise with unattended homes as a listing tool, a marketable skill that sets them apart from their competitors. For many of us, it's easier just to do the job ourselves than to contend with trying to market the home while the neighbor across the street is caring for it. In those situations most of the burden usually arrives back at our doorstep anyway. If it's a tough listing or the listed price doesn't favor an early sale or it's a great listing in the wrong season, the possibility of earning a fee during the delay in transferring the home to a new owner takes some of the sting out of babysitting it. Note this option: Agree upon a custodial fee to go into effect *after* the home has been on the market for the reasonable time it takes for a comparable home in your area to sell.

*   *   *   *

OK, so the owners twisted your arm, thrust a house key into one hand and a garden hose into the other and U-Hauled off into the gathering sunset. Until you bought this book, you couldn't spell custodian and now you are one. But listing custody isn't always the darkest cloud in your career: We can look back on three or four summers of vacant listings with swimming pools, a few winters with spas and several listings with basketball backboards. The attitude around our office is that we owe it to our sellers to put several humans in their pools and splash around from time to time just to keep the chemicals coursing through the skimmers and filters. We will do no less for our clients.

Taking Over

Restoring a note of some seriousness, we've a number of things to talk over with the sellers on their way out of town. A good conversation opener is keys and access.

Obviously, we need the keys, and at this stage, not just those to the front and back doors but everything in the home that has a lock. Heed this warning: This pre-departure meeting may well be the last time you see the sellers or, at the very least, the last time all their property's still in the listing. They're moving, and many things get lost in a move, not the least of which are keys for the home, sheds, gate padlocks, basement and garage cabinets, deep freeze, garbage compactor, circuit breaker box and anything else with a keyway. Grab the garage door Genie off their car visor(s)—it's a key, and won't do them any good in their new home.

Keys suggest access, the topic of the next important question: Who else may have to get into the home, for what reason, ongoing or one-shot entry, and do they have keys? Sharing access and responsibility for a home is unnerving and unfair to the agent—try for sole possession of the place if you can. Few things are more irritating while you are wearing your marketing hat than to drive up to your listing and see a motor home full of your seller's "good buddies" camping in the driveway or finding a strange creature inside, crashed on the floor after a tough day skiing. If it appears that your sellers have a lot of friends with keys likely to drop by, you might want to change the locks. (Possession of keys by others suggests the possibility that a tenancy has been created, intentionally or accidentally. Ask your seller before you call the locksmith.)

*   *   *   *

Before the text gets into the little day-to-day chores that we'll be doing for the owners after they leave, a few questions and decisions remain for their attention. Mail's a good one. A Postal Service Change of Address should be on file, but many owners frequently don't want to file one change to an interim address then refile one for their later, permanent one. We're happy to hold mail for these people or forward it according to their instructions. Ditto for UPS and air express. Newspapers should be stopped, but that's occasionally forgotten in the haste of packing.

Most homeowners have at least one good friend in the neighborhood, and it's nice to know who this person is just in case we get in a jam or need a phone or an ally for any reason. Get his or her name, address and telephone number from the sellers, and drop in and introduce yourself the first chance you get. The motivation is dictated partially by your custodial hat, but it also crosses into marketing. Half the buyers in the world are probably turned onto a home for sale not through a licensee but by a neighbor. A personal relationship with this neighbor can't hurt you a bit!

Cut the Utilities?

A bachelor friend of ours, a bit on the Scotch side, left his home in our custody one summer and went to seek his fortune on the East Coast. He called Sierra Pacific Power, our local gas, water and electricity supplier, and terminated the gas and power. They went for the gold and cut the water as well. And why not? The sprinkling system was on an electric time clock.

All in all, it probably didn't take more than five phone calls, a half-day waiting for the power company to return to turn on services and relight pilots in the furnace and water heater and thirty bucks to switch the account into our office name, all just so we could water the lawn. Counsel clients, whether they are selling to another owner or turning the place over to you, not to terminate utilities—a simple meter reading will be fine. Minimum-use meter charges are preferable to refilling and bleeding air out of water pipes, relighting pilots on gas furnaces and water heaters and doing without electricity for security lighting and evening showing appointments.

Minor notes: If you do cut the power, prop the refrigerator door open slightly to permit air movement and avoid odor. Also, jackets on older water heaters, electric or gas, seem to be prone to fail earlier when allowed to cool down totally and are later reheated. We leave them on; once the water in the vessel's hot, it takes little power to maintain it. Remember that traps in plumbing dry out if left without water for a long, hot period of time, and they eventually admit sewer gas into the home. If the water's to be turned off for any length of time, borrow a bucket of water periodically from a neighbor and refill the traps in toilets, basins, tub and shower and sinks and lavs.

If the owners are pecunious enough to suggest draining and anti-freezing a home during the winter to save heating costs, you might want to decline the responsibility. Draining a home is frequently impractical and portends more trouble than it's worth unless the home was built to be winterized, for example, a mountain cabin.

A fact to remember and to remind owners who want to terminate utilities during showings is that nine out of ten buyers will want to check out the electrical, plumbing and furnace systems in the residence prior to the close of escrow. Termination of utility services during the marketing period will usually result in a reconnection charge before the home conveys, quite probably offsetting the consumption cost saved during the marketing period. Try to convince them just to let the meter run.

Another utility, with a subtle shift, is fuel oil. Natural gas is one commodity; it just keeps coming through the tube as long as someone is paying for it. Oil for the furnace and water heater is a little different—the owners are leaving you with a finite supply, and their heating oil supplier should be advised that you are authorized to order replacement fuel.

The final utility to deal with, and this one you can terminate, is cable TV. That service is frequently forgotten or ignored.

Insurance

Just a couple more questions now, and the owners can go down the highway: Who is the insurance agent and for what company? In the case of an injury to one of your prospects or anyone else legitimately entering the property, or in the case of damage loss to the premises, the burden of working with the agent and adjustors in the owner's absence could fall upon you.

A service available in many communities is the "responsible party" log, maintained in the dispatch center of the police and/or fire station. Some agencies will accept information from any caller; other areas take instructions only from the property owner of record, so this is best handled prior to the owner's departure.

The "responsible" designation ensures that you or your designate will be in the public safety agency's computer and will be notified day or night in the case of an emergency at your client's listing.

A final area for cooperation from your clients might be a signed letter "To whom it may concern," advising the world that you have some status in the operation and care of the property, just in case you have to go to some public agency or a vendor for goods and services for the benefit of the home. The letter might save some uncomfortable or protracted explanations. We're not contemplating a Power of Attorney, which your clients may not want to create (or you may not want to accept) but just a short note, establishing your interest in the home.

Which brings up a point that should go somewhere in a real estate book, and we'll include it here in proximity to the above real-life example: Before accepting a Power of Attorney from a client, bear in mind that you are a salesperson working for the broker, the in-fact fiduciary agent of that client. Existence of and justification for the P of A should be cleared with your broker.

*   *   *   *

We're at a transition in the chapter now—we're alone in someone else's home, maybe the closest person within a thousand miles in a direct position to care for it. Our primary function and reason for our association with the owners and the home is as a salesperson, but in the text that follows we'll tend to discount that relationship in deference to our custodial obligation.

Exterior Care

The obvious duty that comes to mind is mowing the lawn and watering all the landscaped areas of the yard. Since mowing precedes watering, we'll start there with another obvious fact: God gave the breath of life to neighbor kids primarily to help real estate agents clip the lawns of vacated homes.

Most of us have had good luck with the kids, made a few friends in the neighborhood, which can't hurt us a bit down the road, and got the job done somewhat reliably (albeit not a job rivaling the manicuring of the East Lawn, Bushes or shrubs at 1600 Pennsylvania Avenue). But a job good enough to let us show the home without apology was accomplished at a reasonable cost to the owner. The kids can usually tackle the irrigation also, coordinating their mowing around the watering. If the home has a sprinkler system, help them with the valves and intervals, and if there's an electric clock, the work's almost done for them.

*   *   *   *

In more carefree days of yore, we could grab two kids whose folks owned a lawnmower, give them a ten-dollar bill, show them the difference between a ragweed and a Mugho pine and stand back to let them earn some pocket money. A revisit each Saturday morning with a fresh picture of a late president and a couple of milkshakes or a pair of tickets to the Silver Sox at Moana Ballpark would ensure the allegiance of these entrepreneurs for life, or at least the life of the listing.

But times change, and either most of us have grown less carefree in our advancing years or small birds tell us that we've never seen the inside of a courtroom only because we've been lucky, not necessarily intelligent. We now talk to the *parents* of our youthful landscaping teams first, and let their folks assess the kids' skill with power tools. Most parents are still happy to have the children pick up some movie money, but we confer with the parents about reasonable per-mow costs and pay the parents who then turn it over to the kids. It diminishes the pleasure of seeing a child grin at the first ten-dollar bill he or she has ever earned, but the process is more in tune with the legal realities of the late twentieth century.

(We can still bring them an Orange Julius as they toil on a Saturday morning.)

*   *   *   *

Leftover notes about lawns and their watering: Our Oliver Twist theory of child-labor mowing squads applies to uncomplicated maintenance of basic landscaping. If you've listed a home destined for exposure in *Previews* magazine, go for a professional crew. Note two: If you develop an ongoing clientele of vacant listings and have a number of them to keep track of at once, you might want to get a crew of your own together for the summer. Two college kids with a beat-up pickup and a couple of mowers, trimmers and brooms doing work for several real estate agents can easily make tuition for the fall semester.

Spas and Snowflakes

The other two areas of exterior maintenance likely to be inherited by an agent will probably never be a challenge at the same time: Pool maintenance and snow removal.

Pools are prevalent in many parts of the country and can be a striking amenity to a buyer when clean and sparkling. But they don't sparkle easily—a crystal-clear pool usually requires almost daily touching up, even with the best of skimmers and water-jet side and bottom agitators. Labor choices are usually either a pool cleaning service, the aforementioned neighbor kid (same protocol with parents) or, best of all, the licensed real estate agent. Throw a swim suit in your car and do something extra for your clients while you have a little fun for your trouble.

Snow removal is a must for homes on the market for sale, where a procession of strangers may be expected to be coming and going and all are contractual guests in the eyes of the courts. Assess your listing's needs with each snowfall, and clear at least an area for the walkway if not the entire driveway. Our child labor theory fails us here—lawns may be mowed after the "Roadrunner" on Saturday morning, but if it snows Wednesday night and our laborers are in school Thursday morning, we're in trouble. Personal experience tells us that it's about as quick to drive to the listing and clear a path of our own as it is to call around on the phone looking for a snow-shoveling service.

Some would say that few buyers venture out during a snowstorm, so forget the shoveling for a while. Fine, but at least drive in and out of the driveways a couple of times. There's no better giveaway to a vacancy than a pristine Currier and Ives snowfall blanketing a driveway three days after the last storm.

Very few agents will confront snow-removal responsibilities that involve rooftop accumulations on homes and cabins in hard-winter towns and resort areas. Most agents who work these parts of our land know the climate well and have a healthy respect for the will of snow and ice to crush roof structures or slide off the roof and demolish decks and railings below. Clearing roofs is a function of custodial real estate if you're listing a ski lodge, but we don't bring the neighbor kids here on Saturday morning—Tyrolean roof slopes are the workplace of professionals.

First Things First: Marketing!

The balance of the chapter takes us inside the home, where we now put our salesperson's hat back on and try to make the home a little more saleable though now devoid of furniture. What we're envisioning is entry of the home at least twice a week by you or a fellow agent willing to share the responsibility.

Form the habit of looking at door and window locks. Other agents showing the home occasionally leave doors open, and vacant listings in less affluent areas with colder climates are frequently sought out by those looking for shelter from the elements. Run the water once in a while in all the plumbing to keep traps full and Neoprene valve packings moist. If a listing is getting real whiskers, we run the dishwasher to keep the pump vanes and door seals from becoming fatally dry. Check the furnace thermostat; make sure it hasn't been turned to full "off" if that setting is available. If it's a decent day, throw all the doors open for a while and air the home out. Sealed-up homes begin taking on everything from the stale odor of the former occupant's pets to carpet glue to dank crawl space or moist concrete smells, and 20 minutes of air movement does a world of good.

A strange request: Walk into every room of the home and walk around the room once. Reason: Even the best built, wood-floor-joisted home in the land seems to creak if no weight has been put on the floor spanning the joists for several weeks. Under the constant weight of the family's feet, the floor may be quiet for 20 years, but vacate the home for a month, and we'll guarantee an embarrassing squeak when your lead-pipe cinch buyer ambles in.

In some cultures architects laid awake nights to figure out how to make the floors squeak. We visited the 400-year-old palace of Japan's ancestral emperors in Kyoto a decade ago and noticed that the floors squeaked. The informed explanation was that the "nightingale" floor forewarned the royal family of encroachment by assassins. But, if you're marketing a traditional American home to less paranoid Occidental buyers, quiet flooring might be a plus.

Bookkeeping

Our final advice for an agent taking on a custodial listing is to make a strong commitment to bookkeeping records. This is a natural adjunct topic to the earlier chapter devoted entirely to recordkeeping, but we're relocating the material for you to read here while you're all keyed up to list a promising custodial property. Our suggestion has a double-barreled thrust: The first is the necessity for recordkeeping of funds disbursed to others, such as the neighbor kids, the fuel oil company, possibly a utility supplier or a handyman making a repair. The homeseller may realize a tax advantage from these expenditures or may be compensated for them by his or her employer. Accurate custodial records are vital.

The second half of the suggestion addresses the path of money spent for maintenance, and two options are usually available: We might spend our own money and later be reimbursed by our sellers, or, the preferable option, the seller leaves funds with us for the upkeep of the home.

In the latter case, many agents have been trapped by the realization that these funds left behind by the sellers and replenished periodically are, in fact, trust monies held for the benefit of the principal and not to be comingled with our own operating account. In practice, when a relatively small amount of money is being handled for one seller to one vendor of services, hopefully for a short period of time, most agents tend to handle the funds on a personal, albeit business-like basis. But the practice, however minor and infrequent, still deserves the attention of your broker. As funds are managed for more homes and principals and as the amounts increase and time drags out, we recommend that those funds be placed in your broker's trust account and disbursed in accordance with your state's statutes.

*   *   *   *

The definable thoughts on vacant listings and custodial responsibilities now diffuse into a thousand paths that the care and feeding of an unoccupied home can follow, all of which could fill a book ten times this size. The thoughts above are common to almost all such listings and form a springboard that we hope will excite you to develop relocating sellers as a clientele. They're a significant segment of our homeselling public, and all too often their needs and sensitivities, and the care of their homes, are handled by agents as a second priority to occupied properties.

The agent who isn't afraid to roll up his or her sleeves and drag a hose across a yard can solidify an early relationship with relocation-prone employers' personnel offices and get a quick foothold on this productive source of business. Or, if such an agent only lists one vacant property a year, he or she can at least do the job right.

11

Duties Your Exam Left Out

In our town there lives a family by the name of Byars. (Check it out in our phone book: Marv and Tosca.) Also in our town is an ad exec by the name of Sellers (Silas). The Byars owned a home just this side of palatial. One day they put it on the market for sale, and we offered to sell it commission-free if we could interest Si in the home, then take our favorite escrow officer an order wherein the sellers were the Byars and the buyers were the Sellers.

Solomon himself would tangle that escrow up before it closed.

* * * *

The drift of this chapter is to remind us all that real estate can be enjoyable, but we'll throw in a tip or two to preserve a facade of some educational value.

And some of the segments are less for recreation than for sheer interest—try this, circa 1977, for a challenge they never taught you in real estate school:

You picked up a lead from a referral, and arrangements were made for you to visit the sellers in their home. You were told that the homeowners are deaf and mute and that a friend of theirs who can sign would join you at the home to facilitate communication.

What you weren't told was that the couple was in the process of divorcing, and two minutes into the appointment it became evident that it wasn't going well at all. You watched 30 fingers flying through soundless conversations, interruptions and squabbles, and occasionally you detected a lightning-fast gesture that you'd seen before, frequently, on a crowded freeway. The meeting, from the ethical and practical standpoint, was stalemated. You requested your translator to reset the meeting and to prepare the sellers for a larger group of people when you reconvened.

*   *   *   *

The root problem was communication and total absence of the doctrine that we know as a "meeting of the minds." In a normal transaction life pits the sellers against the buyers, and somebody hires a broker to function somewhere between an expert and a referee. At this listing appointment both of the aggressors were on the same side of the fence—a buyer in the living room with you might have been as welcome as a breath of fresh air. And you, the licensee, were incapable of participating in the proceedings.

Difficulty with communication is not an uncommon challenge to real estate agents—this situation was made a little tougher because we were unable to talk to either seller directly. The reality that the sellers were at one another's throats and that our translator might be a friend of one but not of both elevated to unprecedented proportions the conceivable ethical and legal grief that could arise out of such a transaction.

We'll tell you how this situation was resolved and the job got done. But first we'll put this type of dilemma into a more prevalent scenario: Think language barrier. Amerslan (American Sign Language) is a recognized language in its own right, as well-defined as any foreign tongue. And, like many foreign languages, Greek to many of us. Think in that context as we wrap up the story.

A crowd reconvened at the sellers' home, about five strong. Present were their signing friend, two more qualified signers (one assigned to each spouse) and a real estate broker/friend as a witness. We abated the digital fisticuffs, then conducted our usual listing activities, involving appraisal and counseling. Until things calmed down between the sellers, we insisted on concurrence between all the signers as to the tacit counseling and responses. The transaction smoothed out, we found a buyer and had at least two signers present as the offer was presented, accepted and marched through escrow. The transaction closed—we earned our commission on that one, but it was a rewarding and educational experience.

Language

Don't be bashful about going for help if there's the slightest hint of uncertainty about the course of a transaction due to a language barrier. Agents in our area, and we understand in other areas where language varieties are prevalent, have developed a trove of resources and agencies to provide disinterested translators. Obviously, a bilingual real estate licensee (or one who practices signing) is well-postured for success in a nation where Lady Liberty lifts her lamp for so many immigrants.

*   *   *   *

Real estate agents fall heir to a duty that almost supersedes their traditional highest and best use of showing and selling property. We spent 15 years unknowingly fulfilling this duty for clients—it's an insidiously subtle task, one we all do without being conscious of the effort. But it took a trip out of our hometown to a beach community in California, and an afternoon with a real estate broker there, to realize how a fish out of water (the client) feels.

All of Laguna Beach consisted for three previous summers only of a rented condo, a beer purveyor and a mile of sand so far as we were concerned. But as home ownership beckoned, our field of vision widened. The agent spent most of her time telling us not of homes, financing and the usual stuff of real estate but informing us about shopping, commuting, local newspapers and libraries—she became a one-person chamber of commerce, Welcome Wagon and tour director. Heck, we'd seen houses before, and if we liked one, we'd know it. So let's cut to the important things, such as those she was talking about.

*   *   *   *

Since that afternoon, we've had many opportunities to see our own home-showing practice in that new perspective, and our counsel to a newer licensee might be to hone your awareness of your own hometown to the same sharp edge as your purely real estate skills. We've analyzed our interaction with out-of-town buyers and have determined that maybe one of every two inquiries people make of us centers around a non-real estate aspect of living in our town. Their question about zoning may be real estate, but the next question about the local symphony or travel time to San Francisco requires just seat-of-the-pants, getting-out-and-being-aware marketing. To form a relationship with these buyers that clicks and leads to a sale, one out of two correct answers isn't enough—you're their scenic window into this new town.

Climate and Weather

Your local climate is an early target for inquiries from buyers relocating into your town, and a small increment of your time showing appointments is usually spent clarifying or dispelling rumors about your local weather. Example: We live in Nevada, where a recent study proved that 87.2 percent of all Americans residing east of Denver "know" that Reno suffers blizzard conditions rivaling a Robert Service Yukon tale from October to March, and that the sand dunes of Las Vegas (the only other town in Nevada, located 27 miles away) are ravaged annually by sun-crazed camels foraging for food.

We tell our clients that our town is midway up the Sierra Nevada range, and we do get a little snow, and the nights can be a little nippy, but for the most part it's a temperate place to live. Las Vegas, on the other hand, a scant 520 miles to the south, is a mite hotter than Reno, and in modern times most of the camels are confined to the ashtrays on the Strip.

*   *   *   *

Misconceptions about local weather are easily handled. Buyers ask about seasons, of which there are four (4), somewhere. Reno enjoys winter, a weekend of spring, and August. Mark Twain used to say that it rains in Seattle occasionally, that winter spends the summer in San Francisco and San Diego has the finest climate on God's green earth. As a Westerner, we know our own turf, but we'll bet that a reader elsewhere knows all the stereotypes of cities in her area. The misconceptions are kind of fun to hear and amuse the clients as we dispel them, but the real benefit we perform is helping them react to the climate of their new town.

Temperature is a big topic. Many Southern Californians immigrate to Nevada each year and seem surprised to learn that ice does not only occur at the surface of a Scotch and soda. The stuff is actually formed by cold temperature acting on water, as water in a birdbath or a garden hose. Or the tanks of a motor home. We educate our clients but learn to laugh with them, and not at them, as they acclimate to the local lore. Once the tables were turned on us: We asked a hardware clerk in Southern Cal the whereabouts of the frost-free hose bibbs. "What's frost?" said he.

*   *   *   *

Humidity is a curious property—in some parts of the country high relative humidity is as aggravating and debilitating as snow may be for others of us. We include it as a possible topic of interest to relocating prospects, particularly when they are new to a town where the humidity is at the other end of the scale from where they last resided.

Visitors to our town from the seacoast or parts of the Midwest notice after only a few days that their skin seems to be drying. Several months after they move here, they'll note that the drying effect spreads to furniture and appliances and that their new home heats or air conditions with a different "feel" than what they were used to.

Conversely, the evaporative (swamp) cooler that worked so well at a high altitude or in a dry climate becomes almost ineffective in lower or damper climes. Some buyers will find themselves spending good money to buy a humidifier to replace the very quality in the air that drove them crazy in their old hometown. And health is at issue— many people have a tough time adapting from dry to damp, and vice versa, for a short time, and some for a lifetime.

*   *   *   *

If health becomes grist for counseling, don't forget altitude. Who better than a real estate sales agent to tell them that Reno is slightly higher than Honolulu? We met a couple in our town who lived here for months before they realized that we're 4,600 feet above sea level. Maybe their real estate agent should have told them—it wasn't his job, according to the state statutes, but in this chapter we're more concerned about being good hosts and building a warm relationship with clients than staying within the strictest confines of real estate broker-age.

If we have a prospect who is eager to mainstream into life in our town, we mention the local altitude. And quite emphatically, if he's just here from Boston and indicates that he might take a 10K jog before signing the final papers at the title company.

School Daze

Your community's school systems, public and private, are a make-or-break topic with many relocating homebuyers—their kids' education is as integral to their home purchase as the number of bedrooms in the homes they tour. We, as agents, better be ready to handle a broad range of questions about the systems.

In times past, schools within most towns were almost homogene-ous in their curricula and the standard of their optimized graduate. Those days are over—all students are not created equally, and most progressive school districts now recognize a variety of "tracks" a stu-dent may take. In many communities the individual student's appro-priate school may be less dictated by the neighborhood theory of old than by the location of the school specializing in the student's area of expertise.

Veteran agents habitually monitor news of the schools. For many of us it's easy, as we're confronted with a daily update every morning over a bowl of Wheaties. But our own kids' input is seldom enough, and we find it necessary to keep an ear to the ground on a more adult level. A support system of teachers and administrators is handy and easy to build. Over the years we've taken some out-of-towners into a few teachers' lounges after school and let them get information about the children's education right from the horses' mouths.

We keep in mind that the price of pollywogs for the nature lab and instruments for the band hasn't gone down any, so we're usually pretty free with the checkbook as a "thank you" for those teachers that help us out so frequently.

A sharp-eyed reader might recognize such a gift for what it is: Valuable compensation, given to an unlicensed person. We salute that reader, and offer the text as an example of the diligence necessary in preventing departures from the states' laws and statutes.

But many of us make such charitable donations to the schools or other entities that help us, not in direct conjunction with a particular sale, but only once or twice a year. And, a piccolo or a pollywog, given to the totality of a school student body and faculty is not an act regarded by state regulators as likely to bring brokerage as we know it to a halt in our lifetime.

Our Local Architecture

We interject a personal note: One of the more pleasurable aspects of real estate for many practitioners is to grow conversant in the architecture of the homes we sell. The text that follows is not written in that context—appreciating architecture and writing about it are two different disciplines. But we reiterate the suggestion made in the earlier advertising chapter to avail yourself of some of the excellent books about residential architecture.

*   *   *   *

The architecture we write of is partially visual style and design, partially construction techniques and the remainder adaptation to local conditions, climate, building codes or other specialized constraints. Continuing the thrust of the last few pages, we tell our new prospects why the homes they are touring appear or are built the way they are and why a modification that they would like to make may not be exactly welcome or effective.

Some architectural constraints may impact the majority of a market area while others apply only in one area of a town and may have no bearing in another. We'll offer a few examples from both categories.

We know of areas where 95 percent of the homes are built on wood-joisted floors, with masonry foundations and earth crawl spaces. Under-floor plumbing, wiring and heat ducting remain accessible. In other areas an equal percentage of residential construction is concrete slab-on-grade, with almost all mechanicals in the ceiling or perimeter walls.

A buyer who grew up in a slab-floor home might be uncomfortable living 30 inches over the dirt visible in the crawl space, until you tell her that seismic conditions, water table, high compaction or humidity dictate joists instead of the concrete slab she's used to. Many cities are nearly all electric or all gas for cooking and drying clothes, or they are heated predominantly by either electric, gas or oil. It's up to us to tell our new friends that the fuel new to them will work, really, and suggest they relearn to cook on the new heat source. Ditto with furnace alternatives—altitude and temperature ranges rule out some systems. At the seacoast, temperatures may vary less than 10 degrees in a 24-hour period; in our town, we might see a 38-degree morning warm to 80 degrees in the afternoon during the spring and fall. Not a great town for heat pumps.

*   *   *   *

We'll not belabor that point, as we're not trying to write a technical book nor do we have the knowledge to sort out localized adaptations from the great Atlantic ocean to the broad Pacific's shore. We are trying only to inspire you to learn a little more about why things were built the way they were in your town. Local buyers understand the town, but your out-of-town buyers will think you a hero/ine if you can help them into their new home with some understanding of the unfamiliar new conventions.

We mentioned a second category of architectural dictums: These are the ones that vary within your town and exist as a result of deed restrictions and Conditions, Covenants and Restrictions (CC&Rs) within a subdivision where you might be showing property. A rule of thumb: As each neighborhood becomes newer and more toney than the one adjoining it, expect to see increasingly more extensive CC&Rs and rules and regulations that a homebuyer must adhere to as a resident. In many locales the buyers will be asked to sign these printed rules as evidence of their cognizance of them, but the escrow process is a poor and tardy time to deal with one more document.

Thus, our advice: Become familiar with the rules of the nicer projects within your market area. The CC&Rs and deed restrictions are of public record, and your office probably has a set somewhere. Be prepared to tell your buyers, the proud owners of two fine Dobermans, that galvanized chain-link fencing is prohibited and that Apollo and Zeus might be staring at four stained-cedar walls in their new run if the prospects buy the home.

Getting Around

A minor duty of ours is to tell the new arrivals of traffic, and a few shortcuts if we're not trying to keep them for ourselves. Like the flag-pole on a military post, some crossroads usually delineate east from west and north from south, and telling your visiting buyers how the streets work might benefit you, too, if they're finding their own way to a showing appointment. Most cities number homes even on the north and east sides of streets and odd on the south and west, or some such thing.

Locals are usually good about helping out-of-towners. We stood on a corner completely addled in Salt Lake City until a nice lady deciphered their well-encrypted street numbering plan. Only then did we realize why that city's system is regarded as one of the best in the nation. And a kindly police officer in Batavia, New York, sensing that we were from out of town, informed us that one doesn't stop and then hang a right turn on a red light in Genesee County, and he was even nice enough to write it down on a little ticket for us.

Hospitality just doesn't get any finer than that.

Jacks and Jills of All Trades

As a newer agent can plainly see, we wear many a hat as a real estate practitioner. Most of the above activity has very little to do with our li-censed activities *per se*—certainly our state real estate bureau would be hard pressed to chastise us for misleading a buyer about the weather or the benefits of a gas dryer. What this chapter sets out to prove is that we can develop our skills in other ways than those cov-ered in the licensing exam books. We learn that we can create a bond with our clients as we show them homes and, most importantly, that we can outshine our competition by fulfilling a need in buyers' minds that transcends rudimentary real estate listing and showing.

*   *   *   *

A simple thought might be to imagine yourself moving to a new town next weekend, then finding yourself wondering who to call to get a telephone, whether the gas, power and water come from the same utility company and where to get cable TV? Where do the kids go to school? What dentist still takes new patients? And what day is the garbage picked up?

The buyers' usual necessities upon moving to a new town are covered in the freebie fliers that many banks, laundries and other bellwethers of the community give agents to hand out to their buyers. We've yet to see one that responds to the true dilemmas of life, such as who can best retune our cars to sea level, what barbershop has college basketball on ESPN and who carries Queen L'eggs in taupe.

That's the turf of the consummate sales agent—most Americans of normal intelligence could, with proper training and prompting, pass the real estate test in a majority of our states. But the agent that's found the best of the best pepperoni and sausage pizza in her town for an inbound, homebuying gourmet—now there's an agent destined for success.

Horizons

JFK was in the White House, the Beatles were stateside and the brash young writer was in San Francisco cutting his teeth in high-rise (or any-rise) property management. "Bring your camera," said The Boss. "We'll shoot the pine tree on the Hartford Building in the morning."

Unstated in that instruction was that the pine tree, Old Glory and young Karl were to be hoisted to a windswept pinnacle 33 stories over the Financial District (the top 12 floors still were open steel framework) to record the traditional "topping-off" of a high-rise tower.

We learned a lesson that morning that has endured a lifetime of the relative difference between "Can do!" and "Why me?"

*　*　*　*

The most grievous disservice that we could do to an agent immersed in an adventure through the tangled jungle of a real estate career would be to write in the one-dimensional, tightly regimented parlance of bonehead real estate. We all learn the business at a grassroots level and move forward, just as we all read Dick and Jane to prepare for agate-print contracts later in life.

And just as Dick and Jane eventually grew up and bought a condo where Spot wasn't welcome, we're now going to move your frame of reference up just a notch also. The course we set in the pages throughout the book was charted for the agent still in her first job—elements of the business that never seem to get reduced to the printed word.

But we'd be selling you short to intimate that all you will do in your first year or so in business will be to sit open houses and follow prospects around with a tape measure in one hand and a manila envelope in the other. Within the next year you'll probably tackle at least a duplex or a residential add-on or a small office or retail building in light-commercial zoning. This book is of people, not of structures, but we want to reveal definitely that there's more upon your horizon than a single-family dwelling.

*   *   *   *

Let's take that single-family dwelling and see how many tanks of an agent's gas we can burn up in running around town to find out whether an insurance agent can use it for an office if he buys it. The rules for this game are that no time will we undertake any activity that requires any license other than our own real estate salesperson's license.

The given is that the insurance person likes the home—its location and price, the access and visibility and the appearance. We've done our job as a real estate agent. Now the legwork beings.

Is the home within a zoning that permits an office? How many parking spaces per square foot of office space will he need—how about outdoor signs (lit or unlit) and dumpsters? A trip to the local zoning office confirms that it's a viable effort. But we'll probably be back to see them again later.

An office conversion prompts a need for a plan view of the home— a drawing of the home, showing all the rooms in relation to the others in relative size, with the exterior doors and nonnegotiables such as plumbing and the furnace indicated. We put on our draftsman hat and do the drawing for the prospect. (This is the first of several instances where a professional will be needed later in the transaction, but a real estate agent with some expertise can save the seller or prospect some money and accelerate the prospect's decision-making process.)

And while we're measuring the home for the drawing, why not measure the exterior dimensions and distances to the property lines and utilities?

It'll need to be done later by an architect, but figure the area available for parking, "hammerheads" (vehicle turnarounds), walkways and the handicapped ramp. And try to stay away from permanent improvements constructed over fuel tanks or gas lines, driveways under

low power lines and a dozen other details that you'll become adept at
in time. If you're in a creative mood, throw in a few new trees and
shrubbery and a possible location for a sign. In many cities landscaping is integral to a building permit.

Public Agency Input

What does your fire department think of all this? If there's a basement,
is it usable by the public without an alternate exit, and do the floor
joists have to be sheet-rocked? That could result in unexpected cost to
your prospect, as could a need for noncombustible exiting steps. The
fire code might require a reporting fire alarm—another cost.

Most agents know inspectors in the various municipalities' building and safety departments who are invaluable in evaluating questions
of the "Just suppose. . ." variety. Some homesellers are a little queasy
about having their property inspected for fear that the sale may not go
through but they'll still be stuck with some mandated repairs.

And still within municipal services, the Ed Norton input: Find
out from the sewer department the effect in your town of converting a
residence, now paying residential fees, to a commercial building.
Your prospect will want to know whether that impact is significant.

Zoning Activity

We'll make a slight deviation in the scenario at this stage of the text.
Let's assume that the home is *not*, in fact, in a zoning that accepts
light office occupancies.

In many communities in America there's a belt of transition,
within which a former home might now be better suited to light office
or retail occupancy. And frequently the real estate agent is best pos-
tured to assist an owner in securing a change of land use. These
changes are usually less than media events and are supported by prec-
edents down or across the street.

A homeowner may request a Change of Land Use action, usually
by a municipal or county council or commission. And in most areas a
real estate agent may assist that homeowner by going door-to-door in
the neighborhood area impacted by the change to stave off misconcep-

tions about the new commercial neighbor. The second opportunity to assist the homeowner is by providing a cogent presentation of the requested change before the council or commission. Do bear in mind that we are not attorneys, and retreat if the proceedings take on symptoms of litigation.

*   *   *   *

We burned a bit of gas during the two or three days it required to get our prospect a clear picture of his options for the little building. The work we did, for the most part, will have to be reconfirmed or drawn by other professionals with other forms of licensure, but the up-side of our effort is that we got a significant number of preliminary questions resolved and we did it pronto. We've nothing against paying another professional (and we will before the insurance agent moves in!), but we hate to run up a big bill only to determine that the transaction is unlikely to conclude. Finally, our prospect is comfortable in making an offer on the home with an informed insight into its viability as an insurance office.

In terms of the offer we write, which is outside the context of this chapter but worth mentioning, we would probably hinge it on securing a building permit from the appropriate body, and were the zoning not appropriate, we'd make the offer contingent upon the *seller* securing the necessary zoning.

Veterans will confirm that property owners in transitional neighborhoods frequently tend to base their price expectation on the commercial properties in the vicinity. Great, if they've taken the steps to enjoy commercial zoning for their own property. If they haven't, let them bear the burden of upzoning it.

We Meet Many Professionals

So in our first light-commercial transaction, early in our career, we became a shade-tree draftsman and a surveyor, met people from municipal planning and zoning and talked to the fire department and the building department.

In another transaction we might have met a few other people from different agencies: Commercial real estate agents and civil engineers/

surveyors soon become well acquainted. Setting property corners is an obvious service—don't forget drainage and topographic questions, help with easements and legal descriptions and matters of ditches, canals and water rights.

We learned much from early visits to an engineering firm, for much of their work product parallels our work in real estate: It gets recorded with your county recorder and is therefore searchable. Most engineers we work with have been happy to show us how we can do our own research and save their skills and bills for the more complex and interesting assignments.

Which perpetuates our goal of saving our prospects and clients both time and money.

*   *   *   *

Now we'll offer an introduction to a profession you needn't wait to meet until your first commercial listing: The court system!

In most areas, and we're tempted to say *all* areas, listings and sales of properties being held in trust for a beneficiary entity are confirmed in open court, and in most (that word again!) cases they are subject to court confirmation, following an invitation by the bench for higher bids.

The selling trust is represented by counsel, who will be present in court to present and respond to the confirmation. But don't be bashful and stay at home, letting the counsel carry the whole burden. Judges have been known to pose some rather incisive questions about marketing efforts, particularly if the offer is for less than court-directed appraisals. It's wise to be in attendance and responsive to those questions. Offers have been refused by judges who just can't believe that the trust's asset isn't worth more money.

But we work with attorneys in many capacities other than trust conveyances. Most of us have an opportunity to provide rudimentary appraisals or simple comparative sale listings from time to time, and a prompt, accurate response promises future assignments. Inventory of assets, usually of a personal property nature and arising out of an estate or a bankruptcy, is an assignment falling to no particular profession, but somebody's got to do it. We know a broker who confirmed that all Hereford cattle look alike when viewed from the rear (while he counted them in transit) and of a saleslady who singlehandedly counted the entire inventory and equipment of a bankrupt lumber yard.

(And a thought needing only brief mention: Lending institutions and accountants are also frequent customers for similar needs.)

Our barrister and CPA friends are excellent sources of business, in that their clientele take them through the gamut of weirdness and necessity, and many of us have survived a slow winter by undertaking stranger endeavors than counting board feet of timber and beef on the hoof.

Don't Be Bashful

As a reader can plainly tell, an agent needn't hang back like a wallflower waiting for a chance suitor to ask for a dance—the sooner he or she jumps into the fray, the quicker recognition in the business will follow. Don't wait for your own first commercial or complex residential opportunity—find one in progress in your office and ask the agents involved if you can do a little legwork or tag along with them and watch.

Hearken to the suggestion in our "records" chapter—start a collection of resources, and make it grow. Every conversation with a city planner about height restrictions and encounter with a highway department brochure on vehicle traffic counts should find its way into this compendium of knowledge.

The benefits are manifest. The first is a heightened sense of self-sufficiency and the realization that 97 percent of what happens in real estate can be done by a lone human with a brain and a knowledge of where to look for answers.

A second benefit is the cultivation of a trove of professionals, all directing potential clients our way. Quite inelegantly stated, few attorneys aspire to enumerate the south end of northbound cattle, and they'd just as soon delegate, or so we've herd. But recognize the point: Professionals refer both the bitter and the sweet. Our friend who counted Herefords probably got a nice listing somewhere down the road. Just to make sure they know we're around, we keep them all on our Rolodex for newsletters and cards in the same form and fashion as any other client.

The third, and possibly most satisfying benefit of a quest for experiences and a roll-up-your-sleeves attitude, is the perception it conveys to clients: *There's no real estate assignment you can hire me to do that I can't handle!*

Who Needs Us, Anyway?

We might have started something with that last italicized comment. As the Notre Dame fight song swells to a crescendo, we see the team of inspired agents head resolutely out the office door seeking clients needing to be rescued, and we sense that we'd better identify enough clients to go around.

This chapter is about horizons—we spent many a semester teaching real estate as if we were in a world full of nothing but single-family residences, and that all humans are buyers, sellers or agents. And we who write of real estate mostly scribble thoughts that echo that same boring planet and people.

This chapter is intended to broaden your horizons a few degrees. The last few pages have offered a short look at structures other than single family and people who neither bought or sold them, nor had a license to help them. Our intent is that you posture yourself mentally to take the controls and fly a little during your first years in the business.

We've aligned with the typical "brokerage" and "agent." And this book's written for agents who've been in the business long enough to know they plan to stay in it. But some agents, having achieved a license and associated with a firm, later discover that they don't like the business. No shame in that—it's demanding and cyclical. Or a health situation or injury slows down an established agent. Many other doors remain open.

A strong point could be raised that we in real estate education do students an injustice by staying too close to the mainstream, residential brokerage salesperson and not exploring more of the peripheral functions of our profession. The rest of the chapter won't overshadow Indiana Jones for suspense, but as we read through the jungle we mentioned in the chapter's opening paragraph, we'll see a few real-estate-educated denizens hanging from the trees or lurking in the backwaters. But they're all friendly—read on.

Appraisal and Value Judgment

Real estate appraisal is most often cited as the prevalent nonbrokerage endeavor within the industry. Traditionally, appraisers fell outside the states' real estate regulatory umbrellas, and any person could offer what was held to be an "opinion of value" to any other person naive enough to pay for the opinion.

In an increasing number of states, the practice of charging a resident of the state for a document constituting an opinion of value has been brought under that regulatory umbrella—credit the appraisal industry itself for enlisting governmental authority to protect the consumer. Universal adoption of appraisal regulation by all states is far from complete, but it is the direction that the industry's taking.

The appraisal discipline is broad indeed. The "independent" or "fee" appraisers are available to any person, firm or court jurisdiction requiring an independent statement of value for real property, expressed as a leasehold or fee-hold interest, for market value or for another specialized purpose and stated as of the date of delivery of the document, for a past date or a date out in the future.

Fee appraisers rarely act as brokers, in an effort to dispel the color of present or future interest in an appraisal. Frequently they belong to an industry trade association, in part to participate in a multiple listing service and benefit from the MLS's sales prices historical data, and in remainder to make a strong statement as to their ethics and solidarity with the brokerage community.

And their fees, while adjusted to the complexity of the assignment, are not directly related to the value of the property under appraisal.

*   *   *   *

A variant of the fee appraiser network nationwide is the in-house appraiser—another attractive opportunity for real estate licensees (although they're exempt in many states from licensure inasmuch as they do not perform their services for the public). A licensee's background and training, however, are invaluable.

The in-house appraiser typically works for a lending institution and applies techniques similar to independent appraisers to determine value of property under consideration as collateral for the lender's loan portfolio. The in-house appraiser facilitates the loan process by being conversant with the lender's format and by providing the appraisal on a timely basis. (Fee appraisers, you'll come to know, are not known for swiftness.)

Following the fee and in-house appraisers are those independent appraisers approved for government-insured or government-guaranteed loans and government employees performing those appraisals. The inference here is obviously VA and FHA business, but many of the states have their own lending programs for state residents and use the same guidelines, therefore appraisal criteria, as the federal programs.

*   *   *   *

Value determination seems to be big business in America. Here are a few more slots for the sharp licensee looking for an alternate to brokerage.

You could be the person that every homeowner who pulls a building permit for a new hot tub doesn't want to see, known in most parts of the country as the deputy county assessor. Every assessor in the land, while determining value of property taxation, has learned from homeowners that hot tub enclosures, with a cedar bench and trelliage roof, are worth about $75, stained and finished. (For redwood, maybe $82.) This is the same spa enclosure that a salesperson, listing the home for sale, has to get $1,200 extra for or it goes in a Mayflower van at COE.

The various county assessors offices do a bang-up job at property valuation, considering that they work largely with taxpayers who try to kid them and that they work within geographic trends, not specific properties as do their appraiser counterparts.

*   *   *   *

Another alternate to brokerage available to licensees, still remaining in the field of value determination, lies in appraisal of properties under consideration for condemnation by various governmental agencies, utility suppliers and public transportation companies.

In a hostile taking of real property under a right of eminent domain for the public good, a person with tact and diplomacy coupled with a firm background in brokerage and appraisal can negotiate successfully with property owners and cut the time necessary to seize the property while reducing or eliminating the animosity that might endure when the deed is done. And even in the case of an amicable settlement, the cession is a taxable event for the parties, and good backup for the value statement is necessary.

The final candidate for nonbrokerage employment in the value judgment arena is not a full-time job but a short-term nomination. We're speaking of the "arbiter," the disinterested third party required in certain leases and ordered by many courts when two parties are deadlocked on an issue of real property value.

When the kindly judge directs the parties to arbitrate, what she is requesting is one of the many variations of the following: Each party selects a professional, in these cases probably an appraiser. The appraisers, independent of any guidance from their respective principals, select a third party, who shall be known as an arbiter (sometimes "arbitrator") and whose word is law. The appraisers perform their work and submit their reports and the associated supporting documents to the arbiter, who adjudicates the facts, then issues the binding report to his or her principal, in this case the court.

Property Management

Until a decade ago, save for a high level of specialization and expertise in major metropolitan areas, the activity of property management was stepchild to the more important brokerage activity of virtually every real estate office in the land.

Continuing in our discussion of alternative forms of practice, we'd like to sound the word loud and clear that property management has arrived as a skill and industry of its own within the broader real estate family. Within our context of avenues for a newer agent to pursue, we'll confine our thoughts to multiple-residential project management. That invites our attention to the burgeoning number of condominium and apartment projects in America, all of which need professional management. And we'll stick our neck out and bet that there's more residential units coming on line that need management than there are qualified people to fill the jobs.

*   *   *   *

The states are reaching an accord in licensing property managers: The trend is that independent practitioners performing the service as fiduciaries of a project owner/principal shall have a license from their state, which in most cases is considered to be the locus of the managed property and not necessarily the domicile of the management firm.

The alternative to an independent contractor relationship is the manager who is in the direct employ of an owner of a complex. Throughout this chapter we're less inclined to worry about a reader's license status than the opportunities available to any sharp person with a real estate education, so we write with little regard to "independent" or "captive" management.

If density housing has grown in your area as it has in most of the nation, your chances are excellent, as a licensed person, to gain direct or fiduciary employment in a larger complex. The options are typically "on-site," performing duties on the premises, or "resident," having responsibilities on a round-the-clock basis and residing in a unit provided by the owners. A third category, for the employee of an owner holding several properties or as an employee of an independent management firm, is a position in the firm's headquarters office, frequently affording trips out to the various properties to assist, analyze or "backup" the on-site people.

Residential property management is a fairly interesting and seldom boring brand of real estate. We should mention that commercial management endeavors are usually undertaken within the same firms, and while agents are less likely to be involved in commercial projects early in their careers, it's only a matter of time before employees start cross-training.

We make a strong recommendation to any licensees interested in property management to avail themselves of their local chapter of the Institute of Real Estate Management—veterans know it as IREM. It's an affiliate of the National Association of REALTORS®, and IREM members belong to the NAR and ascribe to the same Code of Ethics. Your local chapter can provide more information and the fast-track pathway into management in your area.

*   *   *   *

We remain within property management for a few brief thoughts: Re-read the earlier chapter about custodial listings, if necessary, but picture a large residential brokerage office that might have a dozen or more such listings and a dozen agents who have more to do than go out and backwash swimming pool filters.

The opportunity is the post of brokerage office property manager, a newly created concept in many offices and one that's been around since Day One in others. A licensed person on salary or employed hourly to account for the assets of the office's clients is required.

Also required is the person who may perform one of the last non-brokerage duties we'll include in this chapter: Leasing.

Leasing, in our state and probably yours, constitutes an effort to convey an interest in real property and is therefore held out to be subject to real estate statutes. In most areas it goes hand and hand with property management, and the two terms are spoken almost as one word.

A hairline difference is the requisite for a sense of salesmanship on the part of leasing agents, and that difference often leads to a concept that many who've endured this chapter thus far are trying to avoid: Commission, or some variant of incentive-motivated compensation.

Leasing is big business, and we should all come to know it well as a front-line activity of the real estate industry. As the world gets gobbled up by mega-owners, a leasehold interest in the rock may be as close as many people can come to ownership, residentially or commercially speaking. You may not like the prospect of commission-oriented compensation, but develop a facility for the activity, and keep your knowledge current. It's a reliable fall-back on a rainy career day.

*   *   *   *

The words start to trail off now—we've accomplished most of what we wanted to convey: A few insights that don't get much ink about the day-to-day wanderings we in this business all encounter. And in this closing chapter, a few notes about the alternative paths a sharp agent can take—included as partial restitution for all the nights we taught mainstream "Dick and Jane" brokerage and ignored other major facets of our industry.

There was probably a topic you expected to read about that you didn't find here, and the reason might be that the topic may be a barn-burner in your area only or the topic is so variable around our land that it would require one paragraph per state—a burdensome task to read or write.

We'll include a thought we shared with our students that puts real estate education and practice in the U.S.A. into perspective: If a reader moves from San Diego to Boston, she remains in the same nation with the same Constitution and laws. But should she move a similar distance from Madrid to Oslo, she passes through a half-dozen nations and winds up in a land where the rules are adapted to local practice. We're in one mighty big country, and it's often a tough order to touch all the bases with one paragraph or chapter.

*   *   *   *

The final reason that you might not have read something you expected to find is that the thought is already in another book, *Fast Start in Real Estate*. If you enjoyed this one, you might also find that one amusing and informative.

We ended that last book on a note we find hard to improve upon now:

"And best of all, we had a little fun doing it!"

Index

A

Advertising, 8, 60, 69–78, 88–90: *see also* Self advertising
Affinity farming, 36–38, 39
Anniversary cards, 14
Appraisals, 126–27
Architectural elements, describing, 70–72, 115–16
Asking price, 60
Attorneys, 123–24
Automobile
    of agents, 81–91
    use records, 49–50

B

Backup agents, 93–94
Broker calls, 65
Business cards, 6
Business development, 31–44
    chain reactions, 38–39, 40: *see also* Relocation
    farming, 31–39
Business name, 4–6, 7: *see also* Self advertising

C

Call logs, 61
Cameras, 86–87
Certificate of Fictitious Name, 4
Chain reactions, 38–39, 40: *see also* Relocation

Change of Land Use action, *see* Zoning
Climate and weather, 112-14
Cold calls, 34
Commissions, 19–20: 25–27, *see also* Compensation
Communication difficulties, 110–11
Compensation, 18–29, 95–97
Computerized records, 54
Computer-supported floor systems, 56
Condominiums, in inventory systems, 60–61
Contacts, 38, 39
Correspondence, 12–14
Custodial listings, 98–108: *see also* Property management

D

Daily records, 46–47
Description of homes: *see* Advertising
Direct mail, 12–14
Disclosures, 8–9, 26
Down payments, using commissions, 25

E

Employee relocation, 40–43
Escrow, 21–22
Exterior care, on custodial listings, 104–06